EUROPEAN GENDER REGIMES AND POLICIES

For my daughter, Selma Sümer Mutlu

European Gender Regimes and Policies
Comparative Perspectives

SEVIL SÜMER
University of Bergen, Norway

ASHGATE

Published by
Ashgate Publishing Limited
Wey Court East
Union Road
Farnham
Surrey, GU9 7PT
England

Ashgate Publishing Company
Suite 420
101 Cherry Street
Burlington
VT 05401-4405
USA

www.ashgate.com

British Library Cataloguing in Publication Data
Sümer, Sevil.
   European gender regimes and policies : comparative
   perspectives.
   1. Sex discrimination--Law and legislation--European Union
   countries. 2. Sex discrimination--Law and
   legislation--Scandinavia. 3. Sex discrimination in
   employment--Law and legislation--European Union countries.
   4. Sex discrimination in employment--Law and
   legislation--Scandinavia.
   I. Title
   342.2'4085-dc22

Library of Congress Cataloging-in-Publication Data
Sümer, Sevil.
   European gender regimes and policies : comparative perspectives / by Sevil Sümer.
      p. cm.
   Includes bibliographical references and index.
   ISBN 978-0-7546-7086-5 (hbk) 1. Sex discrimination against women--Europe. 2.
Equality--Europe. 3. Women's rights--Europe. 4. Women--Europe--Social conditions. 5.
Women--Europe--Economic conditions. I. Title.

   HQ1237.5.E85S86 2008
   305.42094--dc22

                                                                              2009014623

ISBN 978 0 7546 7086 5

 **Mixed Sources**
Product group from well-managed
forests and other controlled sources
www.fsc.org Cert no. SGS-COC-2482
FSC © 1996 Forest Stewardship Council

Printed and bound in Great Britain by
TJ International Ltd, Padstow, Cornwall

Contents

List of Tables

Preface

The writing process of this book has been a rewarding and exhausting episode. Even though many people supported me in this project, the actual production of the manuscript has necessarily been a lonely experience. This book coincided with two important changes in my life: My transition to motherhood and the decision of co-residing in Turkey and Norway by commuting between Bergen and Istanbul. These transformations and this book project have interacted and marked my life in the past three years.

Many thanks to the Department of Sociology at the University of Bergen for providing the institutional support for this project. My colleagues in Bergen have always been supportive and enthusiastic about this book. Thanks to Kari Wærness for her support throughout my whole academic life in Bergen and for her valuable comments on parts of this book. Many thanks to Liv Syltevik and Bente Nicolaysen for their care and encouragement. Thanks to the former Chair, Ole Johnny Olsen, for giving me responsibility for the course The Scandinavian Welfare Model and Gender Relations. My experience with that course since 2002 has been one of the major pillars of this book. Thanks to the current Chair, Olav Korsnes, for supporting this book project and offering me the flexibility I needed to teach and write in two countries.

Special thanks to Ann Nilsen for including me in the *Transitions* research team as a postdoctoral fellow. My experience in this EU funded research project has been another major building block of this book. I acknowledge the contribution of the whole *Transitions* team for the data and analysis presented in Chapter 5. Many thanks to Suzan Lewis, Janet Smithson, Julia Brannen and Maria das Dorres Guerreiro for their cooperation.

My family in Istanbul deserves a special thank you for bearing with my book obsession and providing me the back-up and care I needed in the whole process. A special thank you to my mother, Alev, and my aunt, Dilek, for taking such good care of my daughter. This book is dedicated to my little daughter Selma and I hope that she will not need to dwell on gender equality concerns, as much as I did, when she grows up. And finally, thank you Erkan for believing in the importance of this book and for reminding me as well when I occasionally drifted away.

Chapter 1

Introduction

The traditional gender contract is dissolving and is being replaced by a variety of new arrangements between women and men with respect to the gendered division of paid and unpaid work. This is taking place throughout Europe, although with varying form and pace. The last three decades witnessed significant changes in women's participation patterns in the public sphere, producing—and being produced by—transformations in European family practices. The male breadwinner/female housewife family model is becoming a minority practice, while the dual-earner family model is increasingly becoming the model family underpinning various national welfare state and European Union (EU) policies. The vision of social inclusion promoted by the EU involves, at least on paper, a democratic family and a more balanced division of working and caring among women and men.

A fairer distribution of paid and unpaid work is increasingly acknowledged as indispensable in achieving gender equality and social inclusion. Supporting parents in reconciling their work and family responsibilities is stated as a major goal on the European social agenda. Yet, the progress in this field is slow and marked by steps both forward and backwards.

Women's and men's behaviour and expectations related to their participation patterns in education, politics and the labour market have been changing rapidly. Fewer women are prepared for a life-long commitment to home making and more men are questioning the definition of their masculinity only as related to their breadwinning functions. However, structural patterns based on traditional gendered assumptions, allocating different rights and tasks to women and men continue to prevail. Contemporary women and men are facing both new challenges and traditional constraints throughout their life courses.

Despite important developments, comprehensive gender equality is a goal that remains on paper in many European countries. I conceptualize gender equality as a situation in which women have a fair deal concerning their life chances; a social condition in which women and men are not constrained by expectations and structures assuming a certain biological trait. Gender equality is a multi-dimensional and complex phenomenon and there is not one straightforward formula that would work in all social contexts. In the framework of this book, the emphasis is on gender relations in the labour market and work–family reconciliation. Other important gender-equality issues, such as violence against women and trafficking, are necessarily bracketed out. The focus on working parents is guided by the insight that inequalities become especially visible when mothers (re)enter the labour market. This is in no way meant as a privileging of heterosexual couples in relation to other forms of family practices and intimate relationships. The gendered division of work, both paid and unpaid, has been very slow to change and continues to disadvantage women. The labour markets and intimate relationships are organized by differing, and contrasting, principles and the demands of workplaces and families tend to clash. Reconciling work and family pose different problems for men and women and this is gradually acknowledged as a central issue with respect to social inclusion and gender-equality at the level of the EU policy.

This book will focus on these issues with a comparative perspective. It has a European perspective but limits its in-depth analysis to the Scandinavian region and case studies from the UK and Portugal. It tries to present a general view of changing European Union policies on gender and how these operate in selected local settings. Three overarching questions guide the analysis and discussions in this book: What are the key "public issues" and "private troubles" (cf. Mills 1959) of our times with respect to changing gender relations, family practices and welfare state policies? How can we analyse the relationship between the gendered division of paid work and unpaid work with a comparative perspective? Why is there a growing interest in work–family reconciliation at the EU policy level?

A brief biographical account will help to place the production process and the themes of this book in context.

A Biographical Frame

This book stems from my experience as a researcher and lecturer who has been interested in comparative studies of gender relations, family patterns and welfare state policies with a European focus. My specialization in the field of sociology has been based on comparative studies of different scope. This comparative orientation is related to my personal experience of belonging to two countries, Turkey and Norway, and co-residing in two cities at the reverse margins of Europe, namely Bergen and Istanbul.

I completed my first Bachelors degree at Boğaziçi University in Istanbul and travelled to Norway in 1990 with a scholarship for a Masters degree in sociology. Since the day of my arrival, I have been engaged in observing and contemplating the institutional and cultural differences between Turkey and Norway. Despite the similarities in urban living arrangements and university environments, certain areas were strikingly different. For example, almost half of the members of the Norwegian Parliament were women, and gender issues ranked high on the political agenda. When I had to decide the subject of my Masters thesis in sociology, the choice was easy: I would study women's societal positions in Norway and Turkey comparatively (Sümer 1996). My positioning in the two countries as concurrently an insider and an outsider was the essential factor that enabled me to mobilize the "sociological imagination" (Mills 1959) to compare the dynamics of these two societies.

A key finding of that first comparative study, which was based on qualitative interviews with women with higher education, was that Turkish and Norwegian women conceive gender differently (Sümer 1998). While Norwegian interviewees revealed an awareness of gender as a key social category, most Turkish interviewees did not think of gender as a major determinant in their lives and displayed weaker "gendered" identities, conceptualized as a significant sense of belonging to the category of "women" and an awareness of gender as a major social divide.[1] Yet, despite clear differences in terms of their gendered experiences, young Turkish and Norwegian women with a university education, expected to face similar problems related to the conflicting demands of motherhood and employment and to gendered division of domestic and care work. The available solutions for these problems, however, were fundamentally different in each country. The public support offered by the welfare state in Norway—especially the long parental leave; a focus on fathers' leave; and subsidized day care institutions—helped women in combining their earning and caring commitments. On the other hand, the traditional family relations and the availability of affordable household help enabled modern Turkish women to combine employment and motherhood without challenging the conventional role patterns within families (Sümer 1998: 124).

In light of these findings concerning young and educated women, I formulated the research questions for my doctoral project. I continued to investigate the complex relationships between gender, family practices, and state policies through comparative analyses of historical developments, statistical trends, official documents, and face-to-face interviews. Social practices of a specific group—dual-earner, professional couples—formed the basis of the comparative approach in that extended study (Sümer 2002).

My interest in the field of comparative welfare state and social policy analysis focussing on gender was initiated by empirical work. While I was intending to compare Turkey and Norway in light of different theories of late-modernity and individualization, in the course of empirical analysis, the theories of welfare regimes and gender regimes turned out to be more suitable and informative. Theoretically, I moved in to the field of comparative welfare state and gender policy

---

1 In that study, I underlined the importance of using the term "gendered identity" instead of the more familiar term "gender identity" to imply a recognition of plurality and the tension between the term "woman" as a theoretical construct and "the realities of 'women' who may or may not share a unified gender identity" (Marshall 1994: 112).

studies and conceptualized Turkey and Norway as representing different "gender policy regimes." The comparative analysis showed that the prevailing ideology underlying the family policies in Turkey could be labelled "familialistic" since the assumption that childcare and eldercare can and should be met within the family (i.e. by women) led to low public provisions. Norway, on the other hand, could be characterized as an "individualistic" and "de-familializing" gender policy regime, since the state provision for childcare and eldercare was increasingly based on the assumption that both women and men will participate in paid employment (Sümer 2004: 363).

These earlier comparative studies of Turkey and Norway formed one of the pillars of the intellectual base of this book. Another is related to my teaching experience at the University of Bergen. In 2003, I started teaching a course with the title *The Scandinavian Welfare Model and Gender Relations* at the University of Bergen. I planned to structure the theoretical framework of the course around the conceptual scheme of Gøsta Esping-Andersen and the feminist critique of his work. In the process of forming the course syllabus, I collected different articles and book chapters in this field and realized the lack of an update book bringing together both the recent feminist assessments and Esping-Andersen's emerging response to this critique. From my class-room experience, I recognized that presenting this dialogue between Esping-Andersen's original comparative framework and selected feminist critique has a pedagogical value and provides a good starting point for an in-depth study of the field of comparative gender analysis.

Another major building block in the production of this book is my experience as a postdoctoral researcher in a large international research project funded by the Fifth Framework Program of the European Union with the title *Transitions: Gender, Parenthood and the Changing European Workplace* (2003-2005). This project enabled me to extend the scope of my comparative approach and study the dynamics of gender relations with a specific focus on work–family reconciliation, in different European countries (Sümer et al. 2008). The major findings of this international project and an in-depth analysis of work–family experiences in Norway, the UK and Portugal is the theme of Chapter 5 in this book.

Upon completing my postdoctoral project, I started planning the possibilities of combining working and living in Turkey and Norway. After the 15 years I had spent in Norway, during which I kept my ties to my home country both professionally and personally, I was feeling attached to both the city of Bergen and Istanbul. In the spring of 2006, I started co-residing in the two cities, working part-time in both countries. I spent 3 months in a beautiful old house in Arnavutköy by Bosporus in which the proposal for this book was produced.

A key factor that influenced the production process of this book is my own transition to motherhood. The writing inevitably came to a halt several months following the birth of my daughter in January 2007. I took on the work with the manuscript in the summer of 2007 from my home office in Istanbul. I recognized that my perspective on the gender issues at hand was both widened and slightly altered based on my personal, first-hand experience with motherhood and work–family reconciliation. This, I believe, enabled me to analyse work–family policies and practices with a sharpened insider's perspective.

Another particular feature of this book is its perspective on European Union policies. As a sociologist belonging to two countries that both have a unique relation to the EU, I sought to develop a standpoint that combined an insider and outsider view. Turkey and Norway are on the reverse margins of the EU both geographically and symbolically. Norway declined to become a member of the EU following a referendum in 1994 and a majority of women voted against membership, fearing the loss of the already established policies on gender equality. Yet, the relationship of Norway to the EU is characterized by close contact and cooperation through binding economic and social agreements. An important field of cooperation has been gender equality and the Norwegian government has officially declared that cooperation on gender research is a priority area (the Norwegian government's European Policy Platform). Norway participates in various EU funded research projects and implements a range of EU policies internally. Turkey, on the other hand, is a distressing candidate country, facing a massive resistance within the EU and a rise in EU-scepticism internally. A more positive approach to the influence of EU on gender issues characterize the general opinion in Turkey. Major women's organizations in particular see this as an important opportunity to bring gender equality concerns on to the political agenda. My research and personal experience in these two specific contexts influence my approach to the EU gender policies with a view from the margins, while my professional experience as a researcher in an EU funded project provides the necessary insight from within.

Before proceeding with a further contextualization of the theme of this book by providing some facts and figures from the wider Europe, I will first provide definitions for the key concepts at hand. This will also enable me to position the theoretical perspective applied in this book in the general field of sociology and social theory.

Definitions of Key Concepts

As a first step in clarifying the sociological concepts applied in this book, I visit a key dualism underpinning most classical theories, namely agency vs. structure. Following Anthony Giddens' formulation in his now outdated, but still influential, structuration theory, I conceptualize individuals as "knowledgeable agents" who have the capacity of reflecting on their actions, though this knowledgeability is always bounded by the "unconscious" on the one hand, and by "unacknowledged conditions" and "unintended consequences" of action, on the other (Giddens 1984: 282). This conception of agency informs the understanding of "structure" as not something external to individuals, but as "the *medium and outcome* of the reproduction of social practices which it recursively organizes" (Giddens 1984: 25, my emphasis). I believe this clarification is an important first step in any sociological analysis of the relationships between individuals and structures, helping one to avoid the traps of voluntarism and determinism.

In the context of late modernity and high capitalism, European social agents are divided by the still powerful social variables of class, gender, age and ethnicity. Keeping an eye on all these mechanisms, this book focuses on one of them, namely gender, to contribute with empirically driven theorizations.

Gender

Gender refers to socio-culturally constructed components attached to each sex and a basic insight of feminist theory is that these social definitions of biological sex have an important part in organizing social activity. Gender is a concept that is developed and brought to the centre of social theory by feminist thought. It is actually misleading to refer to feminist theory in singular since feminists do not form a homogeneous group. They are divided concerning the way they approach questions related to women, their natures, relations to men and reasons for their disadvantageous positions. There are many classifications within the feminist thought which makes talking about "feminisms" viable (Humm 1992, Hekman 1990). However a usage in singular is instrumental in the feminist political project in which finding common denominators to unite and mobilize women is a crucial task.

The most important advance in feminist theory is that the existence of gender relations has been problematized and that gender can no longer be treated as a simple, natural fact (Flax 1990). Feminist theory seeks ultimately to understand the gendered nature of virtually all social relations, institutions and processes. In feminist approaches, gender relations are not viewed as either natural or immutable. Rather, the gender-related status quo is viewed as the product of socio-cultural and historical forces which have been created, and are constantly re-created by social agents, and therefore can potentially be changed by human agency (Wallace 1989: 10). In this book, gender is conceptualized as a category of sociological analysis referring to manifold processes and relations that generate and sustain structured inequalities between women and men.

This book has a general feminist perspective in which the analysis of the institutional mechanisms by which women end up being less visible in the main decision making and economic bodies and consequently possessing less power (and capital) is specified as a major task. This analysis must be carried out with a simultaneous attention given to divisions of labour both inside and outside the households. Another key task is dissolving the public/private dichotomy and revealing the hidden mechanisms that function to dismiss gender issues from the public agenda by treating them as private problems.

This standpoint endorses a feminist approach that is attentive to historical and cultural diversity, which does not "falsely universalize features of the theorist's own era, society, culture, class, sexual orientation and ethnic or racial group" (Fraser and Nicholson 1990: 27). The focus is on the historical creation of the gendered division of labour and an articulation of everyday experience to historically situated socioeconomic and cultural formations (cf. Marshall 1994).

The social vision embraced by this theoretical stand conceives gender as a key social variable recognizing that "the lives of women and men are cross-cut by several other salient social divisions, including class, 'race'—ethnicity, sexuality and age" (Fraser 2000). It is attentive to massive variation among groups of women and men. The vision for change demands that social life should not be organized "assuming" a certain type of gender difference and that the sex one is born in should not be a major force determining one's life course and chances. It conceptualizes gender equality as a matter of justice, believing that change is possible through collective action. It has an interest in influencing policy making, believing that "the point is to change the world, not simply to redescribe ourselves or reinterpret the world yet again" (Marx, quoted in Hartsock 1990). In this perspective, the welfare state is seen as a major stakeholder and a possible partner in the struggle for this vision.

This note takes us to a clarification of the terms welfare state and the family as two major sites of the construction of gender and power relations. A detailed account of how these spheres interact will be further developed in Chapter 2.

Welfare States and Gender Regimes

The conceptualization of the welfare state in this book is a broad one, underlining the ways states intervene to reallocate life chances, "as a (re)distributor of money, time and opportunities as they play out across the life course" (Daly and Rake 2003: 41).

The concept of "social rights" as formulated by T. H. Marshall (1964) is useful in understanding the bases of the modern welfare state. Marshall had distinguished three types of rights associated with the growth of citizenship: Civil rights refer to the rights of the individual in law, like freedom of speech and religion, right to own property. Political rights refer to rights to participate in elections and to stand for public office. Social rights refer to the right of every individual to enjoy a certain minimum standard of economic welfare and security and include such rights as sickness and unemployment benefits. In most societies social rights have been the last to develop based on the achievement of civil and political rights. The broadening of social rights is the foundation of what has come to be called the welfare state in Western European societies since the Second World War (Marshall 1964).

A basic distinction can be made between marginal and institutional welfare states (Esping-Andersen and Korpi 1987: 40). While the marginal model is premised on a commitment to market sovereignty, the institutional model sees the welfare of the individual as the responsibility of the social collective. The future of the welfare state in Europe has been a contested terrain. As the developments in the social policy agenda of the European Union demonstrate the European welfare state developed as a distinctive solution to the problem of securing social integration within competitive capitalism (Taylor-Gooby 2001).[2] The recent decades witnessed many arguments claiming that the welfare states in Europe would converge in a "race to bottom" (Greve 2007). Several studies show a type of convergence, but not in terms of less social spending. On the contrary, most of the traditionally weak welfare states of the Mediterranean region had to level up their social transfers as a result of EU legislation. Despite worries and predictions, comparative analyses continue to show that welfare states in Europe are not contracting (Taylor-Gooby 2001).

This book is concerned with analysing the major policies influencing gender relations in European welfare states. The state is conceptualized as the central institutionalization of gendered power and each state is seen as having a definable "gender regime" that is linked to the wider "gender order" of the society (Connell 1990). A gender regime is defined as a complex of rules and norms that create established expectations about gender relations, allocating different tasks and rights to women and men (Sainsbury 1999: 5). Gender-sensitive welfare state analysis is built on the recognition of the interaction of gender and class and is linked to a more general critique of the dominant conception of citizenship that ignores gendered processes (O'Connor 1996).

Welfare state's activities in relation to gender is wide reaching, including family, employment, population and housing policies; organization of mass education and regulation of sexual behaviour. The state is therefore a focus for the mobilization of interests that is central to gender politics (Connell 1990, 2002). It is also vital to underline that the state is constantly changing, gender relations are historically dynamic and consequently the state's position in gender politics is not fixed.

Family policy is a field in which the welfare state's ability to intervene into gender relations becomes unusually visible and the public/private dichotomy comes to the fore.

---

2 These developments will be reviewed and discussed in Chapter 4.

Family Practices

Transformations in families and gender relations moved to the centre of social theory from early 1990s onwards. As powerfully put by a key figure in the field: "Among all the changes going on in the world, none is more important than those happening in our personal lives—in sexuality, relationships, marriage and family" (Giddens 1999: 51).

In this book the plurality in the form of families is recognized and family relations are conceptualized as "sets of practices which deal...with ideas of parenthood, kinship, and marriage and the expectations and obligations which are associated with these practices" (Morgan 1996: 11). The term "family practices" conveys a focus on both everyday activities and regularities and it stresses the active rather than the passive or static (Smart and Neale 1999). Family practices include various activities, such as endless negotiations between men and women centred on the housework, decisions concerning if and when to have children and how to arrange their care (Sümer 2002). As David Morgan stresses, "the Janus-faced character of everyday life—looking to both self and society at the same time—is seen or constructed in its clearest form in the case of family practices" (Morgan 1996: 193). This conceptualization enables one to stress that paid work constitutes part of family practices, since it influences the organization of care responsibilities, and provides a fruitful nexus for studying the interactions between the private and public spheres.

In this book, the changes in families are seen as resulting from a basic incongruency in the design of modernity that prescribes the public-private dualism and a traditional gendered division of labour. As Beck and Beck-Gernsheim (1995) have convincingly argued, the prescribed gender roles are the basis of industrial society, and not some traditional relic which can easily be dispensed with:

> Without a distinction between male and female roles there would be no nuclear family, and without nuclear family there would be no bourgeois society with its typical pattern of life and work...On the one hand a wage-earner presupposes a house-worker and production for the market presumes the existence of the nuclear family. In that respect industrial society is dependent on the unequal roles of men and women. On the other hand these inequalities contradict modern thinking and give rise to more and more controversy as time goes on (Beck and Beck-Gernsheim 1995: 24).

Transcending the Public/Private Dichotomy

A key task for a critical feminist perspective is to question and transcend the public/private duality. As Barbara Marshall (1994) argues a basic undertaking for a "critical modernist" feminist project is to make gender visible in the dualistic categories which underlie most theories of modernity:

> The changes associated with modernity—such as the separation of the family from wider kinship groups, the separation of the household and economy…and the emergence of the modern state—are all *gendered* processes. The roles which emerged alongside the differentiation of the economy and the state from the household—worker, citizen—were (are) *gendered* roles (Marshall 1994: 9, emphasis original).

This involves a focus on the gendered division of labour, which is actively created and recreated in both the public and private spheres.

For the sociological classics, the key focus of analysis has been the nexus of relationships brought about by industrial capitalism: Namely, the increasingly specialized division of labour, expansion of science and technical rationality, economic dominance of wage labour and commodity production. The theoretical gaze was directed at the visibly public realms of economics and politics, where "modern man" emerged (Marshall 1994: 27). "Modern women" were mainly thought as conveniently placed inside the home. The public/private dualism was established.

The public–private distinction that many classical sociological and political theories rest on is not unitary; rather it comprises a complex family of oppositions (Weintraub 1997). For example, in the liberal–economist model, "public" refers to state administration, while "private" implies the market economy. Most classical approaches see public in terms of political community and citizenship, while feminist approaches conceive of the public/private distinction as referring to the one between the family and the larger political and economic order (Weintraub 1997). I employ the concepts "private sphere" and "public sphere" in this sense: The former refers to the sphere of the family and intimate relationships, while the latter refers mainly to the state, market economy and the labour market. Whether we look at the division between paid and unpaid labour, or patterns of divisions within paid and unpaid labour, gender persists as the main organizer of work (Marshall 1994). Gendered divisions of labour are not remains of the past; they are actively created and re-created both in public and private spheres. Theorizing the interaction between the two spheres contributes to clarifying the central place of care work in social reproduction.

Care

A key contribution of critical feminist thinking to mainstream sociology has been a fine-grained analysis of the concept of "care." Scandinavian theorists in particular have been active and vital participants in this field (e.g. Wærness 1987, Leira 1992).

Caring is a relational concept which encompasses a range of human experiences which has to do with feeling concern for and taking charge of the well-being of others:

> Whether we analyse caring as 'labour' or as 'love,' it seems highly important to make a theoretical distinction between caring for dependents; caring for superiors; and caring in symmetrical relations (Wærness 1987: 211).

In all European societies, the division of care work is gendered: Women have more of the responsibility for care. Women predominate in caring professions and in domestic care services. Societies and corporations throughout the world have been "free-riding" on caring labour provided mostly by women, unpaid or underpaid (UNDP 1999).

Caring labour that is providing for children, the sick, the elderly, as well as all the rest of us, exhausted from the demands of everyday life is an important input for social reproduction. However, the market gives few incentives and few rewards for it as "the logic of the market runs up against the logic of care" (Wærness 1998: 223).

Daly and Lewis (2000) elaborate the concept of "social care" to identify how care as an activity is shaped by and in turn shapes social, economic and political processes. This concept treats care as an activity and a set of relations lying at the intersection of state, market and family (and voluntary sector) relations (ibid.: 296). Understood this way, the concept of social care leads to a more encompassing analysis of the gender dimensions of social policies and gains a potential to capture trajectories of change in contemporary welfare states:

> For if care is becoming increasingly problematic given that the demand for it is growing at a time when the supply is diminishing, welfare states play a crucial role in mediating the dilemmas just as care creates new dilemmas for welfare states (Daly and Lewis 2000: 296).

To reiterate the feminist position based on these conceptualizations it is vital to underline that this perspective seeks to transcend the public/private dichotomy with its historicizing and comparative focus and perceives care work as a crucial aspect of social citizenship (Siim 2000). It is concerned with differences among women and men and is attentive to other significant social divisions, including class, race, ethnicity, sexual orientation and age.

This approach puts emphasis on the role of men in the project of establishing a more just division of power and develops the vision that a radical change in gender relations must entail a change in men's involvement in care work and in the image of an "ideal worker" as a character free from family obligations. This is similar to the vision originally formulated by Nancy Fraser as the "universal caregiver" model in which women's current life-patterns, that is combining breadwinning and caregiving, will be the norm for everyone (Fraser 2000: 25). This vision is also shared by Esping-Andersen who notes that "ongoing change in gender behaviour is producing an increasingly 'masculine' profile on female biographies...The egalitarian challenge is unlikely to find resolution unless, simultaneously, the male life course becomes more 'feminine'" (Esping-Andersen 2002: 70). This idea at the same time implies that the proposed changes will eventually benefit men as well since a gender-fair society organized this way will be a better place to live for everyone. These assertions concerning the road to gender equality will be discussed in detail in different chapters of this book. What kind of a methodological approach does this specific theoretical position imply?

On Methodological Pluralism, the Comparative Method and Reflexivity

A key methodological characteristic of the theoretical stand sketched above is a firm decision to transcend the qualitative vs. quantitative dualism and to combine methods in light of the specific research question at hand.

Traditionally, comparative researchers tended to rely either on the "synthetic approach" of the historian or on the representative approach of the survey, since it seemed necessary to use techniques that would embrace whole societies (Bertaux 1990). Because of this tendency, little attention has been paid to the use of the so-called qualitative techniques in international studies. This started to change in the 2000s. Hantrais (2005) argues that European funding for collaborative research has stimulated development of an international social science teamwork model in which the pressure on scientists today is "to work qualitatively and quantitatively" (ibid.: 403).

The belief in the intrinsic worth of comparative research is also an element of the theoretical position that strives to activate the sociological imagination. Mills had asserted that "comparative work, both theoretical and empirical, is the most promising line of development for social science...and such work can best be done within a unified social science" (Mills 1959: 138).

The analysis in this book can be characterized as a case-oriented comparative research which aims at understanding and interpreting the diverse historical experiences and institutional characteristics of societies as "macrosocial units":

This knowledge provides the key to understanding, explaining and interpreting diverse historical outcomes and processes and their significance for current institutional arrangements. Most comparativists, especially those who are qualitatively oriented, also seek to interpret specific experiences and trajectories of specific countries. That is, they are interested in the cases themselves, their different historical experiences in particular, not simply in relations between variables characterizing broad categories of cases (Ragin 1987).

Taking the promise of the "sociological imagination" seriously results in a methodological sensitivity that is specifically attentive to historicity, cross-cultural comparisons, and reflexivity. Reflexivity is understood as having two different, but combined levels: The reflexivity of the individual sociologist, as an awareness of her specific social position; and the reflexivity of sociology "in the sense that sociological knowledge spirals in and out of the universe of social life, reconstructing both itself and that universe as an integral part of that process" (Giddens 1990: 16). As argued by Bourdieu and Wacquant (1992), reflexivity entails the systematic exploration of the unthought categories of thought which delimit the thinkable and predetermine the thought, as well as guide the practical carrying out of social inquiry:

Reflexivity is what enables us to escape delusions by uncovering the social at the heart of the individual, the impersonal beneath the intimate and universal buried deep within the most particular (Bourdieu and Wacquant 1992: 44).

Another methodological principle guiding the approach in this book is a belief in the merits of an interdisciplinary analysis. The theoretical orientation sketched above conceives the divisions between the social science disciplines as unproductive, hindering the stimulation of the sociological imagination. Since the promise of the sociological imagination is the hope to understand what is going on in the world by grasping the intersections of history and biography within a society (cf. Mills 1959) all disciplines that have human beings as their subject matters are intimately related. The overarching aim in this book is to provide a sociological analysis of changing gender policies and practices with a comparative perspective. This subject matter is inherently interdisciplinary, located in a crossing field of sociology, comparative politics and social policy.

The focus of this book is the changes in gender relations and different politics influencing these transformations throughout the 1990s and continuing in the 2000s in Europe. The book has an ambition of understanding the local changes in light of the policies initiated or adopted by the European Union. The analysis of the national contexts, however, had to be selective. The book is limited in scope but aims to propose a specific way of combining qualitative and quantitative methods. I draw on both data analyses completed by others and contribute with new empirical data obtained through an international project I personally participated in.

Why is the theme of this book, namely changing European gender policies and practices, significant approaching late 2000s? Let us briefly review the key trends in Europe to elucidate the research questions at hand.

European Gender Relations: Key Trends in Europe

The increasing employment rate of women is a clear and general trend in Europe which influences gender relations both in the private and public spheres. In 2006, a great majority of European countries had more than half of their female population in the labour market. This figure was above 70 per cent in the Nordic countries. The European Union average for female employment rate was 57.6 per cent in 2006 (Eurostat). The targeted rate for the EU is 60 per cent and there are various policies aimed to achieve this goal.

Women's participation in the labour market is still characterized by a high share of part-time employment. The EU average for part-time working women was 31.4 per cent in 2007, with a great variation among countries. Share of part-time working women is only 2.3 in Bulgaria, while this figure reaches to 74.9 per cent in the Netherlands (European Commission 2006b). The pay gap between women and men (difference between men's and women's average gross hourly earnings as a percentage of men's average gross hourly earnings) was 15 per cent in the EU-27 (EC 2006b). Only 32.6 per cent of all managers in the EU were female in 2006 (EC 2006b).

Parenthood has a significant effect on women's participation in the labour market and their working hours. Employment rate for women aged 25-49 without children was 76 per cent in 2006 in EU-27. This drops to 62.4 per cent for women with children. Having children has the reverse influence on men's employment rates, leading to over 10 per cent increase (from 80.8-91.4) (EC 2006b). Women's employment patterns are closely linked to the number and age of their children.

The common understanding today is that women's disproportionate share of domestic and caring tasks is directly related to inequity in the labour market. The definition of the "double day" or "second shift" (Hochschild 1989) of paid and unpaid work as a social problem is an achievement of feminist work. It is now widely accepted that the relationship between the distribution of care work and gender inequality may be challenged through specific public policy (Stratigaki 2004).

A noteworthy demographic trend in Europe is below-replacement fertility rates, showing significant regional variation (Castles 2003). The Nordic countries (together with Ireland and France) display the highest rates in Europe (fluctuating around 1.9) while Mediterranean, Eastern European and Former Soviet countries

Table 1.1   Total fertility rates in selected European countries

	1995	2000	2006
Denmark	1.80	1.78	1.83
Sweden	1.73	1.54	1.85
Norway	1.87	1.85	1.90
United Kingdom	1.71	1.64	1.84
France	1.78 (1998)	1.89	2.00
Ireland	1.84	1.89	1.93
Germany	1.25	1.38	1.32
Portugal	1.41	1.55	1.35
Spain	1.17	1.23	1.38
Slovenia	1.29	1.26	1.31
Greece	1.31	1.26	1.39

Source: Eurostat.

all display rates below 1.5 (see Table 1.1 for details). A brief discussion of changes in family patterns in general will help to contextualize this phenomenon.

A strong trend in Europe overall is the increase in one-person households, that is in solo living. This trend is associated with an individualization of the life-course and a move away from multi-generational households (Daly 2005b). Another key trend is a decline in marriage rates, accompanied by increasing divorce rates. There are regional variations in the prevalence of divorce rates. Southern countries are displaying lower (but increasing) divorce rates. A similar development throughout Europe is an increasing variation in the composition of families, with a general increase in "new family forms" as cohabitation and single parenthood (Daly 2005b). At this point, it is important to underline the fact that although European families tend to display similar trends, countries are moving at their own pace and important differences persist:

> One must, at the minimum, draw attention to the fact that Europe has (at least) two kinds of pattern in relation to family composition and structure. These tend to follow (loosely) a North/South continuum. In Northern European countries, especially Scandinavia, in comparison to those further south more people live alone, average household size is smaller, marriage is less common and alternative living arrangements more diverse and prevalent (Daly 2005b, 383).

Several studies indicate a north–south differentiation in Europe in terms of family policies and fertility behaviour:

> In Northern Europe, children are now born in high numbers whereas marriage has lost its grip; in Southern Europe children are born in low numbers whereas stable marriage prevails. In countries where welfare policies are oriented toward

female employment, where little religious control prevails, and where men have little control over parenthood, fertility will be higher; the level of extramarital births will be higher. In countries where welfare policies are not oriented toward female employment, where strong religious control prevails and where parenthood is more controlled by men, fertility will be lower; births will be marital (Jensen 1999: 11).

Throughout Europe, women are increasing their labour force participation but many are facing serious problems, especially following their transition to motherhood. Women's rising participation in employment, ageing population and family instability put pressure on the European welfare states (Daly and Rake 2003: 168). There are many discussions concerning how to provide good care for children and the elderly and about the optimum public–private mix for care.

There has been a shift in the policy logic of the most European welfare states from a male breadwinner towards an adult worker model that aims to integrate all citizens on the labour market, including mothers. This has politicized the paid work/care nexus and opened new possibilities to place care on the agenda (Hobson, Lewis and Siim 2002: 11).

The traditional gender contract within the families has been changing yet nowhere in Europe are the tasks of caring and housework shared equally. Recent data from Eurostat document the wide gap between men and women with respect to time used in domestic work: Women (aged 15-24) in EU used an average of 113 minutes per day for domestic work, while the corresponding time used by men was 52 minutes (Eurostat 2008).[3]

Analysing data from European Social Survey, Lewis et al. (2008) show the variation among EU countries with respect to actual and preferred working hours and childcare arrangements. Their analysis results in three overriding messages:

> Fathers want to work much less; mothers want to be employed, for the most part long part-time of full-time hours; and in most countries mothers want to have a wide choice of hours, presumably to fit their different and changing domestic situations (Lewis et al. 2008: 33).

Working hours and availability of part-time options are significant factors in understanding work–family practices and preferences (Boje 2006). As Crompton (2006) also underlines, most women seek to achieve a kind of "balance" between paid work and caring work. How this balance is achieved will depend on a range of factors including the general social policy context (influencing the availability of childcare), occupational and geographical constraints and normative

---

3   Based on national time use surveys in the period 1998-2004.

prescriptions as to acceptable family and employment behaviour. Welfare state policies throughout Europe are changing in interaction with the developments at the EU level. The EU is increasingly becoming a major stakeholder and a key actor to focus on in analysing changes in family practices and gender relations. The following structure is constructed in order to focus on these issues with a comparative perspective.

Structure of the Book

Chapter 2 aims to offer a comprehensive theoretical framework for comparative analysis of gender relations and policies. It will start with a review of the work of Gøsta Esping-Andersen on comparing welfare regimes and the selected feminist critique it triggered. The chapter will discuss the recent gendered theory of Esping-Andersen in order to propose a synthesis of the discussions in this field.

Chapter 3 will review recent developments with respect to gender equality in different Scandinavian countries. This is important since the Nordic countries are customarily seen as forerunners with respect to gender equality policies and their instruments for promoting gender equality have inspired recent legislation in the EU. In the Scandinavian welfare regime the ideal of social equality includes an ambition of achieving greater equality between men and women. The chapter will focus on both the major accomplishments and the remaining challenges on the road to gender equality. The Norwegian gender policies and family practices will be analysed in detail as a case study at the end of this chapter.

Chapter 4 will focus on gender policies of the European Union. This is a significant theme since the issue of how EU policies could contribute to developments in gender equality is a major topic of discussion in many European countries. The concept of work–family reconciliation and the strategy of gender mainstreaming will receive a special attention. Various feminist evaluations of these topics will be highlighted.

Chapter 5 will present new data drawn from a EU funded international research project with the title *Gender, Parenthood and the Changing European Workplace* in order to analyse the policies and practices related to work–family reconciliation in different contexts. The social circumstances in the UK, Portugal and Norway will be explored more thoroughly based on organizational case studies and qualitative data.

The concluding chapter will consider the interconnections of the arguments developed in the former chapters. The book will end with a discussion on the possibilities of changing the gendered status quo through European Union legislation, focusing on the challenges of designing flexible and universal policies that would be suitable for different groups of men and women.

Chapter 2
Comparing Gender Regimes: A Theoretical Framework

Comparative analyses of gender relations and studies of different welfare and gender regimes have been fertile and dynamic fields of theory and research throughout the 1990s and into the new Millennium. The interactions between the public and private spheres, which have been widely ignored and marginal earlier, increasingly received more attention from both mainstream and feminist researchers. The demands of the changing realities of individual women and men and growing needs for innovative social policy, together with an increasing cross-fertilization between different schools of thought have been main factors behind this development. In this chapter, my aim is to briefly summarize the theoretical developments in this field to reach a working synthesis.

The work of the Danish social scientist Gøsta Esping-Andersen on the comparative analysis of welfare regimes has been a key contribution in this field leading to many interesting criticisms and reformulations. Esping-Andersen's approach has been a starting point for various feminist scholars who aimed to gender different dimensions of his analysis of the three welfare regimes (Esping-Andersen 1990 and 1992). A number of feminist researchers developed different theoretical frameworks for a gender-sensitive analysis of the relationships among states, markets and families. This stream of research has been the area of one of the most active conceptual developments during the 1990s (O'Connor 1996). What is inspiring in Esping-Andersen's work is that he actively responded to this critique and focused more thoroughly on gender and welfare production within the household in his later publications (Esping-Andersen 1999 and 2002; Esping-Andersen et al. 2001).

I choose to structure this chapter around the selected feminist critique of the work of this former "mainstream" theorist, since this has been an interesting and productive confrontation. This strategy will also enable me to limit the discussion and concentrate on selected topics in order to be able to produce a synthesis that will be a fertile theoretical framework for comparative analyses of gender regimes and policies. I will briefly introduce his original framework and summarize selected feminist scholarship in direct confrontation with this approach. I will then examine how Esping-Andersen himself responded to this massive critique. It is important to note that this is not meant to be an exhaustive summary. The works introduced in this chapter are selected for this specific purpose and many contributors in this field are necessarily excluded.

The purpose of this review is to outline a theoretical framework which will be useful for a sociological analysis of the impacts of welfare state policies on the gender order of a given society. The details of the policy programs and their various economic dimensions are not discussed. The key question guiding this review is: What are the differences between different welfare models with respect to their gendered outcomes and how can these be analysed comparatively?

Comparing Welfare Regimes

Esping-Andersen's approach in formulating his original "three regimes" model (1990, 1992) is based on a critique of linear approaches to welfare states which focus solely on certain indicators (of social spending, democracy, etc.) with the hope to find a single cause of welfare state variation. He underlines that in comparing welfare states, we have to think in terms of social relations since power, democracy and welfare are all relational and structured phenomena. The nature of class mobilization, class coalition structures and historical legacy of the institutionalization of political behaviour are important factors in understanding welfare state variations.

Esping-Andersen bases his analysis of welfare regimes on T. H. Marshall's proposition that social citizenship constitutes the core idea of a welfare state and identifies three key principles involved in social citizenship[1] (Esping-Andersen 1992: 105):

- **Decommodification:** To what extent is distribution detached from the market mechanism?
- **Social stratification:** What kind of a stratification system (class structure) is promoted by social policy?
- **State, market (and family) relations:** Does the state responsibility begin only when the market and the family fail in providing services?

In this scheme, decommodification refers to the degree to which social rights permit people to make their living standards independent of pure market forces. Decommodification strengthens workers vis-à-vis employers and increases their capability of collective action. The variability of welfare states reflects competing responses to pressures for decommodification (Esping-Andersen 1990: 37). A good example for decommodifying social benefits would be sickness insurance, which

---

1   As we will see in this brief review, 3 is a magic number in Esping-Andersen's approach since his analyses tend to specify three dimensions of variation for different principles, leading to three welfare regimes in the final analysis.

guarantees benefits equal to normal earnings, with minimum waiting period and for the duration that the individual deems necessary (Esping-Andersen 1992: 107).

Three sets of dimensions are specified in order to operationalize decommodification: Rules that govern access to benefits (eligibility rules and restrictions on entitlements); levels of income replacement and the range of entitlements provided. Analysing the degree of decommodification in old age pensions, sickness benefits and unemployment insurance in 18 countries, Esping-Andersen argues that the welfare states cluster into three distinct groups (ibid.: 51). He finds a very low level of decommodification in the nations with a history dominated by liberalism and high level in the social democratically dominated welfare states. The continental European countries occupy the middle group.

In a similar manner, Esping-Andersen identifies the salient dimensions of social stratification and constructs cumulated scores for "conservatism" "liberalism" and "socialism" which show a similar clustering. Incorporating an analysis of the interplay of private and public provision in his conceptual scheme Esping-Andersen sets out to analyse welfare states as an aggregate.

Welfare state regimes refer to clusters of distinct welfare states characterized by different arrangements amongst state, market, and family that are reflected in the character of programs (targeted or universal), the conditions of eligibility, and the quality of benefits and services (O'Connor 1996). Based on the dimensions briefly reviewed above, Esping-Andersen identifies three different regimes: Liberal, Conservative/Corporativist and Social Democratic.

The liberal regime is based on "residualist" logic, meaning that the state intervenes only when the market fails. State intervention is subordinate to the market and benefits are means-tested and modest. Entitlement rules are strict and often associated with stigma (Esping-Andersen 1992: 111). In terms of the main dimensions, this regime type is characterized by market dominance; class dualism and minimum decommodification. Typical examples of the liberal welfare regime are the United States, Canada and Australia.

In the conservative regime, social rights are connected to status and class; preservation of status differentials is a main goal. Conservative regimes are also shaped by the church and maintenance of the traditional family is emphasized. The "subsidiarity principle" emphasizes that the state will only interfere when the family's capacity to service its members is exhausted (Esping-Andersen 1992: 112). In terms of the main dimensions, the conservative regime is characterized by a moderate level of decommodification, a primacy of the family and social policy aiming at preserving the existing class structure. Germany, Austria and Italy are shown as typical examples.

The social democratic regime is characterized by high institutionalism, universalism and egalitarianism. Social benefits are based on citizenship and are financed by taxes.

Social democracy was the dominant force behind social reforms. An equality of the highest standards (rather than an equality of minimal needs) was pursued. Universalistic programs are preferred to selective ones. This implies that manual workers enjoy rights identical to white-collar employees or civil servants. High level of decommodification, wide-ranging state responsibility and a goal of promoting an egalitarian class structure result from these principles. This regime is typically exemplified by Scandinavian countries.

Esping-Andersen underlines that it is important to see these models as dynamic and as analytic tools. It is often difficult to find a country which exactly fits into a regime type. Most welfare states have elements of all three regimes and no single case is pure (Esping-Andersen 1992: 113).

In discussing the causes of this clustering, Esping-Andersen maintains that the hope to find one single motor must be abandoned and the task should be identifying salient interaction effects:

> The salient forces that explain the crystallization of regime differences are interactive. They involve, first, the pattern of working class political formation and, second, the structure of political coalitions with the historical shift from a rural economy to a middle-class society (Esping-Andersen 1992: 118).

The "welfare regimes" approach briefly summarized above has been widely discussed among the social scientists (e.g. Cousins 2005, Kleinman 2002). Some used different dimensions and analysis techniques, ending up with the same three regimes (e.g. Powell and Barrientos 2004), others argued for inclusion of alternative regime types, like the "Southern Model" (e.g. Ferrera 1996). While a few argued that there is no empirical evidence for these regimes and that the typologies must be dissolved.

Despite various criticisms, many acknowledge the power of this typology in comparative analysis:

> It enables analysts of social policy to develop a picture both of patterns of difference and of broad directions of change. It allows them to raise their heads above the details of legislative programmes and their implementation in individual countries and to consider the importance of more general tendencies which cut across national developments. It provides a starting-point from which the significance of differences can be explored more fully (Cochrane et al. 2001: 11).

The work of Esping-Andersen was attractive for feminists due to its multi-dimensional and dynamic character. The confrontation between the framework of welfare regimes and various feminist perspectives resulted in an impressive amount of intellectual production and interesting arguments, characterized as "cross-fertilization" by an important contributor in the field (O'Connor 1996). The next section will present a review of some of the main feminist criticisms of this original framework.

Selected Feminist Critique: Gendering Welfare Regimes

In this section, I will present key arguments of selected feminist scholars. Given the vast amount of production in this field, the review inevitably excludes many important contributions. These contributions are selected purposively to underline the major streams of critique which Esping-Andersen responded in his later work. In a report with the title "From Women in the Welfare State to Gendering Welfare State Regimes" Julia S. O'Connor (1996) had provided one of the first detailed reviews of the feminist critique of welfare state analysis. Many contributors in this field agree that Ann Orloff's critique should be treated as a classical work which paved way for other critical studies.

Ann Orloff Builds Gender into Esping-Andersen's Framework

In her article titled "Gender and Social Rights of Citizenship: The Comparative Analysis of Gender Relations and Welfare States" Ann S. Orloff (1993) proposed an alternative scheme for evaluating and categorizing state social provision that can capture both class and gender effects. Orloff followed the strategy of directly engaging the conceptual framework of the "power resources" school in order to transform it to incorporate gender relations.[2]

Esping-Andersen's analytic scheme was developed to answer the question: "How do states affect class relations?" Orloff asked the necessary complementary question: "What about gender? How do states affect gender relations?"

Orloff argues that such concepts as "worker," "citizenship" and "decommodification" are based on a male standard and gender relations and their effects are ignored:

> An accurate picture of the content and effects of state social provision should not begin from the premise of a gender-neutral citizenship. Rather, one must take into account of the real gender differences in productive and reproductive labour

---

2   In this article Orloff focuses on the analytic schemes of Walter Korpi and Gøsta Esping-Andersen as prime examples of the power resources school of analysis.

and access to civil and political rights and how these differences influence the
ways in which men and women struggle for and claim benefits from the state as
citizens (Orloff 1993: 309).

Many institutions and processes that constitute gender relations are directly affected
by state social provision, for example, the sexual division of labour (including the
treatment of care work) and access to paid work. States regulate gender relations
in the labour market, polity, family and elsewhere.

Orloff mentions that the male worker serves as the ideal-typical citizen in the
literature on social rights. Power resources analysis begins with economically
independent citizens and considers the cross-national, historical and class
variations in the ways social rights affect them. They focus on programs that
compensate workers for losses incurred in the paid labour market, such as old-
age pensions and unemployment insurance. The social rights of citizens who are
economically dependent (the majority of whom are women) are not considered.
We need to analyse the different ways men and women claim benefits from the
state as citizens, but the existing dimensions specified by Esping-Andersen and
Korpi (1987) and Esping-Andersen (1990) are flawed and need to be gendered.

Gendering the state–market–family dimension entails recognition of the unpaid
caring and domestic work of women. In the original framework, attention has been
given to division of labour between states and markets and the family dimension
was largely ignored. As Orloff emphasizes, nowhere in the industrialized west can
married women and mothers choose not to engage in caring and domestic labour.
Women carry out a disproportionate share of welfare work, whether it is provided
by the state, private organizations or the family, and to the extent that this work is
undervalued, women suffer disproportionately.

The conceptualization of a "division of labour" among states and markets must
also include families as significant providers of welfare, and the unpaid caring
and domestic work of women must be explicitly recognized. In this framework,
the state can be defined as "woman-friendly" to the extent that policies reduce
the sexual division of labour by shifting the burden of domestic work to public
services and to men (Orloff 1993: 314).

Gendering stratification dimension entails focussing on the effects of social
provision on gender hierarchies. Power resource analysts have not addressed the
significant ways that states reinforce gender hierarchy by privileging full-time
paid workers over workers who do unpaid work (or who combine part-time work
with domestic and caring labour) and by reinforcing the sexual division of labour
in which women do the bulk of unpaid work.

Most women's claims are based on familial or marital roles which often have stricter eligibility requirements and lower benefit levels than direct, work-based claims. According to Orloff, the theory of decommodification is not well equipped to account for women's positions since it is too fixated on the impact of wage labour and neglects the crucial role of unpaid caring work in the welfare state. Decommodification provides workers with income from outside the market. However, the positions of male and female workers in the labour market are different. Women in general do not have the same access to paid employment, and one of the main factors here is their domestic and caring labour. At the same time, benefits that decommodify labour give male workers greater capacity to resist capital and enter the market on their own terms, but unpaid services provided by mothers, wives, daughters also enhance male workers' capacities.

Following these propositions of gendering the existing dimensions, Orloff suggests that decommodification must be supplemented with a new analytic dimension that taps into the extent to which state promote or discourage women's paid employment—the right to be commodified—naming it "access to paid work" (ibid.: 318).

Orloff argues that if decommodification is important because it frees wage earners from the compulsion of participating in the market, a parallel dimension is needed to indicate the ability of those who do most of the domestic and caring work to survive and support their children without access to a breadwinner's income (ibid.: 319). She proposes the inclusion of another dimension to capture this, namely "the capacity to form and maintain an autonomous household." This dimension permits the investigation of the extent of women's freedom from compulsion to enter or stay in marriages in order to obtain economic support.

In concluding her project of gendering the different dimensions of welfare state analysis, Orloff emphasizes that incorporating new dimensions of social provision that consider gender relations will make research more complicated and the newly defined gender regimes may not parallel the three regimes identified by the "power resources" school of analysis. Her prediction has been confirmed by various comparative research projects focussing on the effects of state social provision on gender relations.

Diane Sainsbury's Three Gender Regimes

1990s witnessed different attempts of "gendering" welfare state analysis through a rethinking and critique of Esping-Andersen's original framework. Some of these were collected in a book with the title: *Gendering Welfare States*, edited by Diane Sainsbury (1994). This book is one of the first contributions in the field which aim a synthesis "by drawing on a broad spectrum of insights from *both* feminist and mainstream research" (Sainsbury 1994: 1). The key focus of the different contributions is an analysis of "how the division of labour among the sexes and gender ideologies shape social provision and, in turn, how social policies affect the life situations of women and men across welfare states" (ibid.: 7).

In a following publication with the title *Gender and Welfare State Regimes*, Sainsbury (1999) brings together different contributions that further develop the gendering of welfare state regimes by showing how gender-relevant variations cut across welfare state types.

In a chapter entitled "Gender and Social-Democratic Welfare States" Sainsbury (1999) outlines gender models of social policy emphasizing the importance of gender and familial ideologies as a key variation. Her basic ambition is to analyse the patterning of variations between different welfare models as distinct "gender policy regimes":

> Gender policy regimes can be distinguished on the basis of ideologies that describe actual or preferred relations between women and men, principles of entitlement, and policy constructions (Sainsbury 1999: 77).

Sainsbury bases her analysis of gender policy regimes on four dimensions of variation:

- Whether the rights are individualized or familialized.
- Degree to which gendered differentiation in entitlements is based on the traditional division of labour between women and men.
- Scope of state responsibility for caring tasks.
- Women's and men's equal access to paid work (Sainsbury 1999: 79).

Based on this scheme, Sainsbury specifies three gender policy regimes: The male-breadwinner regime, separate gender roles regime and individual earner-carer regime. In the male-breadwinner regime, men have entitlements stemming from the principle of maintenance, while married women's entitlements are primarily as wives. The separate gender roles regime underlines a strict division of labour between the sexes, but attaches weight to both the principle of maintenance and the principle of care. The individual earner-carer regime envisions greater equality between women and men and "the transformation of the traditional division of labour between the sexes, so that each individual is involved in both caring and earning" (Sainsbury 1999: 260). This gender regime and the social-democratic regime have complementary logics, in that both individualize and thereby defamilialize social rights.

The analyses in this book show the significance of the "interrelationships between systems of income maintenance, taxation, public provision of services, and the labour market in structuring and transforming gender relations" (ibid.: 9).

They also put emphasis on women's activism as a source of policy variations both across and within welfare regimes.

Jane Lewis' Breadwinner Models

Jane Lewis is another feminist scholar who as been in dialogue with Esping-Andersen's original framework, contributing with her own typology of gender and welfare regimes (Lewis 1992, 1997). Focusing on how women are treated in the social security system, the level of social service provision and married women's position in the labour market, she distinguishes between the strong, moderate and weak male-breadwinner models.

In an article entitled "Gender and Welfare Regimes: Further Thoughts," Lewis (1997) reviews critiques of both Esping-Andersen's typology and her own analysis of breadwinner models. She underlines the difficulty of capturing all aspects of differentiation in a single typology and states that the measures will inevitably reflect what is considered to be the most important issue at stake. Following this argument, she specifies two main questions concerning the provision of unpaid work as central for the analysis of gendered welfare regimes: How to value it and how to share it more equally between men and women? (Lewis 1997: 170).

Lewis maintains that to study further the relationship between paid work, unpaid work and welfare we need a new map based on the possible sources of cash and care and how they are combined (ibid.: 173). Referring to McLaughlin and Glendinning (1994), Lewis underlines the importance of thinking about defamilialization rather than decommodification:

> This would clearly encompass how far men and women were to be helped to reconcile paid and unpaid employment, and it leaves room for the idea that the right not to care...might be as important as the right to care (Lewis 1997: 173)

Defamilialization is a concept initially used by feminist scholars as a precondition for their capacity to commodify themselves. As we will see in detail later in this chapter, this is the concept Esping-Andersen draws on in incorporating gender into his conceptual framework.

Critiques Focussing on Culture and Regional Differences

In a book entitled *Gender, Economy and Culture in the European Union*, Simon Duncan and Birgit Pfau-Effinger (2000) bring together different contributions that aim to highlight the regional variations within nation-states. The authors are critical of what Duncan labels "state fetishism" (2000: 16) and try to propose theories that will be more attentive to cultural and regional differences within nations, asserting that "in explaining sub-national differences in gender inequality and the lives of women and men, we need to combine analyses of both economic and cultural relations (Duncan 2000: 20)."

In his introduction to this book, Duncan (2000) reviews various attempts of "gendering the three worlds of welfare Capitalism" and claims that:

> The theoretical core of Esping-Andersen-derived models is firmly rooted in capital-labour divisions...based around the relationship of (male, standard) workers to markets as modified by the welfare state...The explanatory dynamic remains gender blind however much gender description is added on (Duncan 2000: 8).

Based on the pioneering work of the Swedish theorist Yvonne Hirdman on the "gender contract" and Birgit Pfau-Effinger's work on "gender culture" Duncan develops the "genderfare" model. His key aim is to include variations in both the capital-labour contract and the gender arrangement and to theorize gender spatiality at the local level (2000: 16). Pointing at the "spatial amnesia" in social science, namely the equation of spatial differences with national differences alone, Duncan sets out to formulate an approach that can deal with regional differences within countries. Reviewing several studies on regional variations in women's labour force participation, he concludes that:

> Gender divisions of labour are culturally reproduced—even when the economic conditions that may have produced them in the first place are long gone...In explaining sub-national differences in gender inequality and the lives of women and men, we need to combine analyses of both economic and cultural relations (Duncan 2000: 20).

In her conclusion to this collection entitled "Gender Cultures, Gender Arrangements and Social Change in the European Context," Birgit Pfau-Effinger (2000) argues for a more culturally sensitive approach to comparative gender relations analysis. Her aim is to integrate "culture" into a theoretical framework in explaining gender differences cross-nationally. Her "gender arrangement" approach is based on the assumption that gender cultural ideals and values form an important basis for the behaviour of women and men and that the basic social institutions also function on the basis of such ideas. She underlines the fact that cultural values about the central sphere of care for children and elderly vary throughout Europe:

> Should this be mainly a task of the state or, and to what degree, should this be shared by the state and the family? Should women and men share the tasks equally, or should the market mainly provide care? Connected with these ideas about care are differing ideas about the amount of time which women and men —as carers—should spend in employment (Pfau-Effinger 2000: 273).

In my opinion, a focus on "welfare regimes" and "gender regimes" does not exclude cultural factors. Rather, they are built in the theoretical analysis on which the regimes are modelled. The questions related to the primacy of public or private responsibility and to social stratification involve key cultural values.

Mary Daly's Critique of Typologies

Mary Daly is a sociologist who has been a major contributor in this field (Daly 2000a-b, Daly and Rake 2003). She published a book with the title *The Gender Division of Welfare* in 2000 in which she investigated how particular types of welfare state arrangements affect the distribution of resources and opportunities between men and women. In particular, she examines the impact of British and German welfare states on gender relations. Viewing gender as integral to welfare states, Daly claims that the relation between gender and the welfare state is expressed "in the structure or content of relevant policies, the processes to which policies give rise, and the outcomes that are effected by policies" (ibid.: 231). In a contemporaneous chapter with the title "Paid work, unpaid work and welfare: Towards a framework for studying welfare state variation" Daly (2000b) summarizes her theoretical perspective through a review of existing work on the relationship between gender and the welfare state. She specifies three main approaches in the field: Those centred on the concept of care; those using the concept of citizenship and those seeking to construct typologies, especially focussing on breadwinner models. Daly notes that there is little conversation between the three approaches and that "the key challenge is to rework these concepts into a comprehensive framework capable of countenancing variation and complexity in how welfare states embody and affect gender relations" (ibid.: 24).

According to Daly, a comprehensive framework to theorize the welfare state should link together the content of policies, the processes set in train by welfare state provisions and their outcomes. While typologies are useful in analysing the architecture and design of policies, the concept of care "speaks most readily to the processes and relations set in train by the welfare state in telling us how welfare state (and other) provisions construct particular types of labour…as paid or unpaid and formal and informa" (ibid.: 35).

On the matter of outcomes, Daly notes that, while the association of welfare states with equality is problematic it can be assumed that resources (re)distributed through the state will be less unequal than those distributed by market forces and that through its redistribution functions the state effects some reduction in inequality overall. Through these activities the state has a strong shaping hand on resource relations between men and women (ibid.: 36).

The second conceptual task in developing a comprehensive framework is to theorize the welfare states relationship to the family and the labour market, conceptualizing them as interacting spheres:

> Life courses and the wellbeing of both women and men are constituted at the intersection of welfare state, family and market. The essence of the interaction between the welfare state, family and market from a gender perspective is how they constitute and affect paid work, unpaid work and welfare (ibid.: 37).

In concluding her arguments on theoretical concerns, Daly underlines the need for a more plural approach to methodology:

> With regard to comparison, I am of the view that typologizing should be set aside in favour of few countries/many factors type of work…Comparative energies… are best concentrated upon developing concepts and modes of analysis which do justice to the rich detail of welfare state provisions considered in their context. Hence, country case studies would appear to offer a better way forward (ibid.: 38).

In a later publication entitled *Gender and the Welfare State*, Mary Daly and Katherine Rake (2003) develop the conceptual framework specified above and choose eight countries for detailed case studies. The countries they analyse are France, Germany, Ireland, Italy, the Netherlands, Sweden, the UK and USA. The countries are chosen for their diversity, as representatives of a broad range of welfare states (Daly and Rake 2003: 5). They seek an answer to the key questions concerning the extent to which there are national patterns around work, care and welfare and how these are gendered in terms of their processes and effects. Based on a detailed analysis of different dimensions, the authors conclude that although Sweden emerges as a clearly distinct model, there is no easily identifiable grouping of the other countries (Daly and Rake 2003: 161). They claim that typologization risks freezing welfare states in time and underplays differences among countries of a particular type (ibid.: 167). This research also uncovers differentiation among different groups of women, revealing the complexity of gender policy making.

Daly and Rake (2003) underline the problematic aspects of regarding participation in paid work as being equivalent to social inclusion, especially regarding mothers. They also point that "productivist models of welfare" in which all are expected to participate in the labour market, tend to hide inequalities in access to employment (ibid.: 178). They conclude this book arguing that "the success of future welfare states depends upon meeting the varied expectations and demands of women and men as they pursue a lifetime's worth of care, work and welfare" (ibid.: 178).

Seeking a Synthesis

In an article entitled "The Work–Care Balance: Is it Possible to Identify Typologies for cross-national comparisons?" Barbara Haas (2005) reviews the existing approaches in the field of welfare regimes and attempts to create a typology as a tool for analysing what is happening in practice with respect to families' working and caring strategies. Haas identifies two main strands in the field of cross-national studies of gender relations:

> Either researchers have attributed more emphasis to institutional arrangements that support, or hinder, female employment, which is labelled as the 'structuralist' approach, often dealing with different types of socio-political welfare states and breadwinner systems...Alternatively, researchers deal with the importance of individual attitudes. This so-called 'culturalist' approach focuses on gender arrangements, especially on the social values, norms and preferences that go hand in hand with a gender specific division of labour (Haas 2005: 490).

Haas shows the work of Jane Lewis on breadwinner models as the primary example of the structuralist approaches and the work of Birgit Pfau-Effinger as a key example of culturalist focus. Reviewing different "structuralist" and "culturalist" approaches that propose different welfare and family models, Haas (2005) attempts to integrate them in a new theoretical framework to gain a "better understanding of the deeper relationship between the practices, the culture and the policies of the work-care balance" (ibid.: 489).

She underlines the need of an analytical distinction between practices, policies and culture. Practices refer to the empirical outcome of social and care policies, the effective division of unpaid and paid work between genders. Haas emphasizes that the socio-economic situation of the couples, their economic and educational levels "play an important role in understanding the practices in dividing up paid and unpaid work" (ibid.: 494).

Haas emphasizes the need of analysing these topics with a multi-method perspective since cultural norms and attitudes are best illustrated by qualitative open interviews.

> A synthesis of the structuralist and culturalist approaches leads to various new types, covering a wide range of theoretical options with regard to the division of labour between the two genders: Including the traditional breadwinner model, the modified breadwinner model, the egalitarian employment model, the universal carer model and the role reversal model. These types are different from the structuralist and culturalist approaches, insofar as they focus on the compatibility of work and care in partnership rather than on the integration of women in the labour market (Haas 2005: 495).

Presenting findings from a comparative analysis of practices, policies and cultural orientations in Austria, the Netherlands and Sweden, Haas (2005) argues that even though it is possible to identify typologies for the compatibility of work and care, countries may be classified in different models according to the level of analysis and to the time dimension.

As the brief review of selected theories above showed, the work of Esping-Andersen on comparing welfare regimes has triggered many different types of responses and resulted in diverse theorizations. Even those who are not directly involved in criticizing the "Three Regimes" approach, feel almost obliged to refer this productive debate in this field.

Let us now briefly review how Esping-Andersen responded to this massive critique and started to develop a more gender-sensitive approach to welfare state variation.

Esping-Andersen's Work Incorporating Gender Relations

As I mentioned earlier, what is most inspiring with Esping-Andersen's work is his move from a fairly gender-blind position towards analysing welfare states with a gendered lens.

In his 1999 book *Social Foundations of Postindustrial Economies*, which he specifies as an attempt to revisit *The Three Worlds of Welfare Capitalism* in light of numerous criticisms, Esping-Andersen promises to pay more attention to the criticisms regarding his insufficient attention to gender differences and family as a major producer of welfare. He acknowledges that:

> As the notion of a 'second demographic revolution' indicates, and as all statistics demonstrate, the changing role of women and evolving new household forms are an intrinsic—possibly leading—part of the socio-economic transformation around us. Our grandfathers were male bread-winners; our grandmothers most likely housewives. Very few children today grow up in this kind of family. Household forms are being revolutionized even if some welfare states do not seem fully aware of it (Esping-Andersen 1999: 12).

In the chapter titled "The Household Economy," Esping-Andersen revisits welfare regimes through the analytical lens of the family. He provides an analysis of different welfare regimes according to their degree of "de-familialization" defined as "the degree to which households' welfare and caring responsibilities are relaxed —either via welfare state provision, or via market provision" (Esping-Andersen 1999: 51).

De-familialization is a concept originally developed by feminist social scientists referring to policies that lessen individuals' reliance on the family. Hobson, Lewis and Siim (2002: 19, in footnote 4) state that the term has been first used by a number of feminist researchers, including Chiara Saraceno and Ruth Lister before it appeared in Esping-Andersen's work.

Esping-Andersen underlines the fact that de-familialization does not imply "anti-family." On the contrary, it refers to a regime which seeks to unburden the household and diminish individuals' welfare dependence on kinship (Esping-Andersen 1999: 51). A familialistic system is one in which public policy assumes that households must carry the principal responsibility for their members' welfare; hence, de-familialization would indicate "the degree to which social policy (or perhaps markets) render women autonomous to become 'commodified,' or to set up independent households, in the first place" (ibid.).

Underlining the importance of capturing women's autonomy, Esping-Andersen directly responds to Orloff's critique who had suggested the inclusion of this dimension to capture independence.

Esping-Andersen specifies four kinds of indicators to analyse the level of de-familialization: Overall servicing commitment to families, subsidies to child families, public child care for children below the age of three and supply of care to the aged (Esping-Andersen 1999: 61). His analysis shows that the correlation between fertility and women's paid employment is exactly the opposite of what one might expect. Revealing the correlation between high familialism and low fertility, Esping-Andersen moves to a feminist position through an economic argument:

> Contemporary welfare states can no longer count on the availability of housewives and full-time mothers. The more they do so, either by actively encouraging familialism or by passively refraining from providing an alternative, the more they diminish welfare at both the micro- and macro-level. At the micro-level, familialism is now counter productive to family formation and labour supply. This means low fertility, lower household incomes, and higher risks of poverty...At the macro-level, it implies a waste of human capital (in so far as educated women's labour supply is suppressed) (Esping-Andersen 1999: 70).

Esping-Andersen continues to develop his analysis of the gendered dimensions of welfare states building on feminist concepts in *Why We Need a New Welfare State* (2002) co-authored with Duncan Gallie, Anton Hemerijck and John Myles. This book is a revised version of the report "A New European Welfare Architecture" which was prepared for the Belgian presidency of the European Union in 2001. The authors state that the book concentrates on four major life course related issues: Childhood and families with children, gender equality and the compatibility issues facing working mothers, working life and retirement (Esping-Andersen et al. 2002: xxv).

In the chapter entitled "A New Gender Contract," Esping-Andersen directly confronts gender issues. He opens the chapter stating the vital connection between changes in women's societal positions and welfare state restructuring:

> Many regard the fight for gender equality as largely a 'women's affair.' If women are emerging as a key axial principle in the new socio-economic equilibrium, it follows that the quality of our future society hinges on how we respond to their new claims on men, the welfare state and on society at large. For good or bad, gender equality becomes therefore a 'societal affair' a precondition for making the clockwork of post-industrial societies tick. Gender equality is one of the key ingredients that must go into our blueprints for a workable new welfare architecture (Esping-Andersen 2002: 69).

Esping-Andersen states the key question he sets out to answer in this chapter as "what kind of equality and how?" First he makes the distinction between two distinct objectives inherent in the project of gender equality: The first is the issue of harmonizing the dual aims of careers and motherhood and the second one is the aim of full gender neutrality in the allocation of opportunities, life chances and welfare outcomes (Esping-Andersen 2002: 70).

In his analysis of the compatibility problem, Esping-Andersen refers to the heterogeneity of women's preference sets, referring mainly to Catherine Hakim's formulation of the three distinct types of women: Family-centred, career-centred and dual-role models (Esping-Andersen 2002: 72, see also Hakim 2006). Hakim's preference theory has been widely discussed among feminist social scientists (see for example Crompton 2006). Without going into the details of this controversy, I just need to mention that I find Esping-Andersen's uncritical reliance on this "choice" theory somewhat curious because he is a major theorist of structures that function as major constraints on choices.[3] I am also sceptical of too much reliance on the preference theory since preferences are often shaped by what is conceived as available and they tend to vary throughout the life-course based on different opportunities and constraints one faces. With this caveat, it is important to note that later in his discussion, Esping-Andersen has been careful to underline that while on the one hand women's "choice menu" is being revolutionized, on the

---

3   Esping-Andersen's reliance on Hakim's preference theory is criticized by several feminist theorists. For example, Rosemary Crompton (2006) argues that although Esping-Andersen now sees women's economic behaviour as central to welfare state analysis, his analysis still incorporates "gender stereotypical assumptions related to women's 'preferences'" (ibid.: 136).

other hand, "so are the forces that limit citizens' ability to realize their dreams and aspirations" (ibid.: 88).

Esping-Andersen provides a detailed analysis of different aspects of support for working mothers stating that "any serious and realistic compatibility policy must address the combined (and interactive) effects of public support, employment structure, and wage expectations" (ibid.: 73).

He presents an overview of different countries' performance on the basic "women-friendly"[4] policy package that includes adequate child leave entitlements and day care. His analysis highlights two directly opposed trajectories on the north–south axis in Europe:

> The Nordic countries represent a positive-sum scenario in which public support for working mothers coincides with an ample 'mother-friendly' labour market and a wage structure that encourages near universal female employment. In direct contrast, Southern Europe's low fertility rates are testimony to the fact that *all* factors influencing compatibility combine negatively: An almost complete lack of affordable child- and elder-care, unusually limited part-time options, a very undeveloped service labour market, pervasive job precariousness, and also fairly pronounced gender wage inequalities (ibid.: 80).

He then moves on to discuss gender equality across the life course, focussing on gender segregations in the labour markets and the gender pay gap. The consideration of managers' perceptions of the greater risk associated with female employees, resulting in direct discrimination leads him to recognize the issue of the division of domestic tasks, an area which he has been vehemently criticized for ignoring in his earlier work. In concluding his discussion of the new gender contract, he states a vision for change, pointing at the need of a transformation in men's life courses:

> We can abstractly imagine a world in which women begin to embrace the typical male life cycle model, lock, stock, and barrel. In this world there would be almost no children. We do happen to know that men's and women's desire for children remains intact, so this leads us to conclude that there is, realistically, a limit to female life course masculinization. Remaining at the level of pure abstraction, we must conclude that true gender equality will not come about unless, somehow, men can be made to embrace a more feminine life course (Esping-Andersen 2002: 95).

---

4   Another aspect which I find unfortunate in this chapter is his use of the term "women-friendly" without referring to the Norwegian political scientist Helga Hernes who is acknowledged as the originator of the concept (Hernes 1987, and see Chapter 3).

Esping-Andersen has been an important character in the field of comparative welfare state and gender policy analyses mainly due to two complementary reasons: He has been instrumental in bringing originally feminist ideas and concepts (like defamilialization and women-friendliness) onto the mainstream policy agenda. At the same time, his genuine interest in social justice and inclusion led him to develop a significantly gender sensitive approach to welfare state analysis.

Currently, Esping-Andersen is working on a book project with the title *How Women are Changing the World* and the drafts for the different chapters of this book are available on his website at: http://www.esping-andersen.com/. The book focuses on the "female revolution" and its ramifications throughout society. This project confirms the transformation in Esping-Andersen's theoretical orientation form a rather gender-blind towards a highly gender-sensitive position.

Conclusion

The feminist critique of the mainstream theorizing on welfare regimes brought the issue of gendered division of both paid and unpaid labour into the center of the analysis. The centrality of the care work, often carried out within the families by women, is now widely acknowledged. The assignment of differing family statuses and activities to women and men is confirmed as one of the main roots of gender inequality.

Feminist studies analysed how the gendered division of labour shapes social provision and documented the significant production of social welfare in the domestic sphere. Many argued convincingly that the interconnections between the welfare state and gender relations need to be observed in the critical domains of "care, work and welfare" (Daly and Rake 2003).

A common argument of researchers focusing on gender relations is the idea that we should conceive the three key institutions, namely the state, labour market and the family as interacting spheres. This leads to a comprehension that analysing how people organize for care, work and welfare is a critical task in understanding the relationships among these key spheres of life (Daly and Rake 2003). Gender plays a crucial role in organizing both paid and unpaid labour.

How particular types of welfare state arrangements affect the distribution of resources and opportunities between men and women have been analysed thoroughly by feminist scholars. Some of these studies focused on showing inter-regime variations (e.g. O'Connor et al. 1999) while others argued for a move away from typoligizing (e.g. Daly and Rake 2003). A group of feminists are dissatsified with Esping-Andersen's analyses of gender and family changes. For example, Hobson, Lewis and Siim (2002: 12) claim that though Esping-Andersen elaborates the family dimension in his analysis, gendered implications of these changes and the idea that welfare states have different "caring regimes" is missing. Others continue to argue for the usefulness of welfare regimes thinking in analysing broad tendencies. For example, Orloff (2001) argues that even though there are important variations within clusters, some significant gender consequences of overall welfare regime architecture remain:

> The emphasis on state provision of services in social-democratic regimes supports mothers' employment and reconciliation between employment and care. The antipathy to state provision of income or services—and preference for the market...leaves women in the liberal regimes vulnerable to poverty, and reliant on the market for services to support employment (and with no guarantee that the market will provide them). The family-oriented character of the conservative-corporatist regimes constrains women's employment, or forces a trade-off between care/childbearing and employment (Orloff 2001, 82).

Esping-Andersen also endorses a continued focus on welfare regimes in analysing current institutional arrangements in Europe:

> Neo-liberals advocate the primacy of markets (and usually ignore the family), while conservatives favour more family and local community social responsibility. And social democracy's longstanding preference for collective solutions is anchored in its fear that both the family and the market alternative foster inegalitarian results. Europe is indeed an amalgam of ideologically distinct traditions. From this diversity we can learn a lot about which institutional option seems to perform well or poorly in the pursuit of any specified welfare goal. The choice of how to divide the responsibilities between the three cornerstones of the welfare triangle is what scholars term a choice between alternative *welfare regimes*. And it is this, in the final analysis, which we must decide upon (Esping-Andersen et al. 2001: 14).

As the review above made clear, Esping-Andersen now assigns a central place to women's employment in his gendered theoretical framework:

> Female employment is one of the most effective means of combating social exclusion and poverty...'women-friendly' policy is simultaneously, family- and society-friendly...it should, accordingly, be defined as a social investment (Esping-Andersen 2002: 94).

European countries differ with respect to their policy approaches to the issues of gender inequality and family instability and these differences are significant elements forming distinct gender regimes. A gendered analysis of welfare states and policies need to keep an eye on the complex interaction between the labour markets and families—the public and private spheres— and recognize the centrality of women's care work for the general welfare of the society. A key policy issue is to contribute to a valuing of care work and encouraging men's participation in it.

In comparative studies of welfare and gender regimes, Scandinavian countries consistently distinguish themselves as social contexts in which women's favourable representation in the public sphere and their possibilities of combining motherhood and employment are facilitated by different public policies which aim at changing the gendered division of labour. This point takes us to a detailed analysis of the Scandinavian Model in the following chapter.

Chapter 3
The Scandinavian
Gender Regime: Myth or Reality?

As the review and synthesis in the former chapter showed, an institutional welfare state is generally considered as a key actor in eradicating gender inequalities. In the international arena, as well as within Scandinavia, a broad opinion regarding women prevails: Scandinavian women have reached a higher level of equality with men compared to most other European countries, mainly because of the specific design of the Nordic welfare model.[1] Key indicators used to support this assertion are often related to women's high rates of participation in the labour market and politics. The specific welfare model prevailing in these countries is often characterized as the source and outcome of the egalitarian values prevailing in Scandinavia, comprising gender equality as a widely held ideal. We will explore this assertion further in this chapter by reviewing major gender equality policies in Nordic countries and how they operate in practice. Following a general assessment of the social positions of Scandinavian women and gender relations, the chapter will focus on Norway as a detailed case study to analyse the accomplishments and challenges of the Scandinavian gender model.

In this chapter, I choose to downplay differences between Scandinavian countries in order to clarify the common elements of their gender policies. Many Scandinavian researchers have rightly focused on important differences between Scandinavian countries (e.g. Bergqvist et al. 1999, Ellingsæter 2000b) but in the context of this chapter, the focus is on the similarities that become clearer when approached with a wider European perspective.

There are many indicators supporting the general view on the "liberated and equal" Scandinavian women. For example, all the Nordic countries range at the top according to the gender-related development indexes of the UN Human Development Report. Gender Empowerment Measure (GEM) is a composite index measuring gender inequality in three basic dimensions of empowerment —economic participation and decision-making, political participation and decision-making and power over economic resources. Although this approach has

---

1 I use the terms "Scandinavian" and "Nordic" interchangeably although there is a discussion about the inaccuracy of this (Bergqvist 1999). I focus primarily on the three Scandinavian countries—Norway, Sweden and Denmark—in this context. The term "Nordic" usually includes Finland and Iceland as well.

Table 3.1   Selected countries according to GEM rank and women in politics

Country	2007 GEM rank	Parliament (% seats held by women)
Norway	1	38
Sweden	2	47
Finland	3	42
Denmark	4	37
Germany	9	30
France	18	14
Italy	21	16
Portugal	22	21
Greece	37	13

Source: UN Statistics, Human Development Report 2007) <http://hdrstats.undp.org/indicators/279.html>

been widely criticized, especially for ignoring other fields that are important for women's empowerment, I conceive GEM as a useful tool when it is employed to analyse what it intends to measure; namely women's participation patterns in the public sphere. This measure provides figures that enable one to analyse women's public participation patterns different countries comparatively.

The 2007/2008 Human Development Report provides the following ranking by the Gender Empowerment Measure:[2]

1. Norway
2. Sweden
3. Finland
4. Denmark
5. Iceland

It is no coincidence that the five Nordic countries rank at top. Country ranking according to GEM and women's participation ratios in national parliaments show a clear north–south polarization in Europe as documented in Table 3.1. Political representation is a good indicator of women's social power and their collective chances of influencing policy-making.

As we have mentioned in the former chapter, the Nordic countries are customarily characterized as representing the social democratic welfare regime which promotes an egalitarian social policy that encompasses gender equality as a major goal. Before embarking upon a detailed analysis of this assertion, a brief note on the historical development of the Scandinavian welfare model will be useful.

---

2   Available online at: http://hdr.undp.org/en/

The Scandinavian Welfare Model: A Brief Historical Overview

The beginning of the modern welfare state can be traced to Bismarck's large scale social insurance schemes in Germany in the 1880s (Esping-Andersen and Korpi 1987). The compulsory sickness insurance scheme was followed by accident insurance and old age and invalidity pensions insurance. Sweden was the first Nordic country in setting up an investigatory committee to study the German programs, but the laws implemented did not follow this model. The old age pension law which was passed in 1913 went further than any existing national law in the world and included the principle of universal coverage (Esping-Andersen and Korpi 1987). The historical turning point leading to the establishment of the Scandinavian Model came with the Great Depression of the 1930s. The unions and social democratic parties grew rapidly and a stable parliamentary alliance was formed between the Social Democratic parties, representing the working classes, and centrist parties, representing farmers. This political realignment was a major factor leading to the institutionalization of the Scandinavian model (Esping-Andersen and Korpi 1987: 46).

The cornerstones of the modern welfare state were laid during the post-war period. The universal flat rate pension scheme of Sweden was copied by Norway and Denmark in the 1950s. During the 1960s, the welfare model was further institutionalized and the Scandinavian countries moved in the direction of Marshall's social citizenship idea in most of its social legislation (Esping-Andersen and Korpi 1987: 49).

The key characteristics of the welfare model shared by the Scandinavian countries can be summarized by three essential features:

- **Comprehensiveness:** The scope of public intervention is defined broader than in most other nations.
- **Level of institutionalism:** The model does not recognize any fixed boundaries for public welfare commitments since the underlying view is that the welfare of the individual is the responsibility of the social collective.
- **Universalism:** The welfare state is meant to include the entire population rather than target particular program groups. Social policies aim at uniting the population instead of dividing it into "those who get the benefits" and "those who only have to pay" (Esping-Andersen and Korpi 1987: 42).

The 1980s and early 1990s are often characterized as years marking a "crisis" for the Scandinavian Model. Low economic growth and an increase in unemployment led to various rollbacks, especially in Sweden. Norway was least effected by the economic crisis due to vast oil revenues which even allowed for more social investment (Ellingsæter 2000b).

The so-called "work line" that characterized the 1990s involved reductions in benefit levels, shortened benefit periods and tightened eligibility, combined with a stronger emphasis on activation, education and training (Eitrheim and Kuhnle 2000). Yet, despite several cut-backs in social expenditures the Scandinavian countries are still characterized by high levels of social equality and public responsibility in the 2000s. Citizens and legal residents have basic rights of access to a broad range of services and entitlements, including free (or cheap) education and health services, universal old-age pensions and comprehensive family policies. The basic policy logic of the Scandinavian welfare model is state intervention to modify the play of market forces in order to achieve greater social equality (Sainsbury 1999). Active labour market policies to promote full employment; expansion of public services available as a social right and social rights based on citizenship or residence, rather than work performance, are the key tools used by the welfare state aiming to weaken the influence of the market on entitlements (Sainsbury 1999).

As Eitrheim and Kuhnle (2000) argue, there is a persistent stability resting on the institutional legacy of the Scandinavian Model which is apparent in the dominant role of the state and the public sector, the prevalence of the principle of redistribution through general taxes, producing relatively egalitarian distribution of income, and full employment as an overall goal (ibid.: 55).

The model inevitably looks better on paper than in real life. Yet, various comparative studies show that the attempt to develop an ambitious welfare state based on the idea of universalism and equality is not without results (e.g. Kautto, M. et al. 2001; Abrahamson et al. 2005). The reality of the model may not correspond to its ideology in all respects, but neither is it a myth. In a recent assessment of the economic performance of the Nordic model, a group of economists (Andersen et al. 2007) argue that there is a success story of a favourable combination of economic efficiency and social equality and a common finding of cross-country comparisons is that the Nordics succeeded better than other countries in combining economic efficiency and growth with a peaceful labour market, a fairer distribution of income and social cohesion (Andersen et al: 2007: 12). The authors identify the aging population, resulting in a dramatic rise in the dependency ratio, as a major challenge facing the Scandinavian countries but argue that it is essential to preserve one essential feature of the model—collective risk sharing—in responding to the current challenges (Andersen et al 2007: 13).

Various comparative studies focussing on gender and family policies also show that there is a distinctive Nordic pattern despite considerable differences in the economic development patterns of different countries (Björnberg 2006). Let us now turn to a detailed analysis of the Scandinavian way of approaching gender equality.

The Scandinavian Gender Regime

A common feature of all Scandinavian countries is the dominance of the ideal of social equality. There are, however, differences in terms of specific policies and institutions that are set up to achieve this goal. There are also important cultural and political differences between the Scandinavian countries. For example, religion has a stronger influence in politics in Norway, while Sweden and Denmark are among the most secular countries in Europe (see, for example, Borchrost et al. 1999 and Kjedstad 2001 for details of other major differences). In this context, my main aim is to provide a brief review of similarities in the gender equality machinery in Scandinavia that led many observers to talk about a specific model and then focus on the major accomplishments of the Scandinavian gender equality regime, together with the key challenges it faces.

The "passion for equality" (Graubard, referred to in Hernes 1987) prevailing in Scandinavia encompasses a general orientation towards gender equality as well. This democratic culture has been a major factor leading to the strength of the women's movement in the 1970s which in turn had a key role in bringing gender equality onto the political agenda. The feminist movement in Scandinavia mainly targeted equal status for women and men in society, focussing on economic independence for women as a key to achieve equality. The Nordic countries were ahead of the international movement with respect to the power of the feminist research in influencing social policy measures (Haavio-Manila 1981).

The Scandinavian policy of equality in general is based on the assumption that education and economic independence are the two sources from which all forms of social power derive (Hernes 1987). The broad collective mobilization of women in the 1970s played a key role in the institutionalization of gender equality issues through legislation. The system including a wide range of gender equality policies and state institutions with the specific purpose of furthering women's interests and improving their position in the public sphere is often characterized as "state feminism" (Kjeldstad 2001). There are different feminist views on the possibilities of an alliance with the state, yet a good number of Nordic feminists tend to be optimistic and argue that state feminism has improved women's general position, giving them new resources for mobilization and political influence (Kjeldstad 2001: 70).

In the Scandinavian regime, social rights that are granted independent of family relations and based on citizenship or residence weaken the influence of the market and the family on entitlements (Sainsbury 1999: 260). At the same time, expansion of public services provides new jobs and the growing welfare state becomes a major employer for women. The extensive public provision of care services serves to recruit large numbers of women to employment. Sainsbury (1999) argues that the social-democratic welfare regime resembles the "individual earner-carer" regime since both envision greater equality between women and men and aim at "the transformation of the traditional division of labour between the sexes, so that each individual is involved in both caring and earning" (Sainsbury 1999: 260).

There have been contrasting views on the usefulness of using the concept of a gender regime when analysing Scandinavian policies. Kjeldstad (2001) argues that there is evidence for an explicit "Scandinavian Model" in terms of gender equality policies and outcomes. A common feature of the current institutionalized gender equality policies of the Scandinavian countries is that they developed through interplay of commitment from both the top and the bottom, namely an interaction between political elites and grass-roots mobilization.

In order to provide a comprehensive analysis of gender policies in practice, it is important to focus on women as political actors and mobilization "from below" and the effect of women-friendly policies "from above." This is the approach developed by the influential Norwegian political scientist Helga Hernes in her analysis of the *Welfare State and Woman Power* (1987).

The Scandinavian Gender Regime and the Concept of "Women Friendliness"

Recently, several theorists reinvented the term "woman-friendliness" as a useful concept in discussing policies that would support gender equality in the context of instable families and labour markets (e.g. Esping-Andersen 2002). One of the most detailed theoretical accounts of this term was originally provided by the Norwegian feminist social scientist Helga Hernes. According to Hernes (1987) Nordic democracies exemplified a state form that makes it possible to transform them into woman-friendly societies in which gender-based injustice would be mostly eliminated:

> A woman friendly state would not force harder choices on women than on men, or permit unjust treatment on the basis of sex. In a woman-friendly state women will continue to have children, yet there will also be other roads to self realization open to them. In such a state women will not have to choose futures that demand greater sacrifices from them than are expected of men. It would be, in short, a state where injustice on the basis of gender would be largely eliminated without an increase in other forms of inequality, such as among groups of women (Hernes 1987: 15).

Hernes specified three phases of equality policies in Scandinavia. Most policies of gender equality have started out as labour market policies to encourage women to enter the labour market. In the second phase, problems of unequal treatment are addressed, mainly in gender neutral terms of equal access. In the third phase, men are encouraged to take over their share of family work by giving them parental leave. The goal is gender neutrality within the family and society at large (ibid.: 19). Hernes summarizes the changes that took place in women's positions as a result of the effects of both the Women's Movement and the gender equality policies of the welfare state in the following way:

> During the 1970s women entered the labour market, albeit on a part-time basis; they stayed longer in the educational system; Scandinavian men began to participate more in child care, although not in housework strictly speaking; women increased their political participation and representation rates to the highest in the world, although without achieving parity or a majority of seats (Hernes 1987: 20).

Hernes developed the key argument that the division of labour between family, market and the state is decisive for the welfare of women and for their social power. In contrast to many other Western countries where traditional family work has been marketized, the Nordic solution has been its incorporation into the public sector administered by the state and municipalities. The new boundaries between private and public involve the acknowledgement that care for the young and elderly are public concerns (ibid.: 17).

Women's employment in Scandinavia is facilitated by the public take-over of the provision of education, health and welfare services such as day care for children and services for the elderly. This phenomenon has been analysed by Hernes as "the family going public." This term refers to the active involvement of the welfare state in socialization, education, care of the young children, the sick and elderly and to the professionalization and expansion of these tasks. This development is essential in understanding the Scandinavian gender regime:

> The growth of the Scandinavian public sector, which by European standards is heavily skewed in favor of the health and care system rather than public works, has in general been of a magnitude comparable perhaps to the industrial revolution. It is this process that has drawn women into the labour market on a large scale, often on a part-time basis, and affected families and the relationship between the family and the state in a fundamental way. The expansion of the public sector can be described as the family's 'going public'. In terms of number, women now dominate the public sector, and they have monopoly on all service work (Hernes 1987: 135).

The social democratic welfare states in Scandinavia introduced generous systems of leave of absence and invested in public childcare services. These policies improved the situation of working mothers and contributed to an equalization of the situation of women and men in terms of labour market participation. By the same token, the welfare state became a major actor in women's lives. According to Hernes, we can analyse these transformations as a "transition from private to public dependence." While women were dependent on economic support of either their fathers or husbands earlier, they are now economically dependent on the welfare state (ibid.: 31-49). Many women are employed in the public sector and use public childcare services to combine motherhood and employment. However, the relationship between the welfare state and women is not one of partnership but "dependence." Writing in late 1980s, Hernes pointed to three gendered facts in the labour market disadvantaging women: Women still earn less than men on the average as "equal pay for equal worth of work" is not accomplished; a great majority of those working part-time are women and women are few among top management in both labour unions and industrial organizations. These disadvantages continue to persist in the 2000s. High levels of gender segregation characterize the Scandinavian labour markets. Hernes summarizes the negative trends hindering the development of a woman-friendly state as follows:

> Existing difference in women's and men's private and public roles as well as differences in institutional power have helped to develop state and market into gender-specific arenas for action, to maintain the family as women's major responsibility in terms of work, and to the development of strongly gender-segregated labour markets (ibid.: 136).

The concepts developed by Hernes in 1980s have been used extensively by feminist researchers analysing the relationship between gender relations and welfare state policies throughout 1990s. The "empowerment hypothesis" arguing that welfare state can be an instrument for improvement of women's rights and positions challenged the dominance of feminist theories that dismiss any alliance with the state. Nevertheless the concept of women-friendliness has also been criticized by feminist scholars for being culturally biased towards the Nordic countries and for underestimating continuing gender hierarchies (Borchorst and Siim 2002).

The concept of "women-friendliness" and Hernes' analysis of the relationship between women and the welfare state received a renewed attention in the 2000s and guided various studies on gender policies in Europe. Women's representation in politics and the labour market and their opportunities for combining motherhood and employment take the central place in Hernes' analysis. Let us now look at the major developments in Scandinavia related to these fields.

Scandinavian Women in the "Public Sphere"

Political power of women is a key indicator for women's possibilities to influence policy-making and legislation. In a comprehensive study of the relations between gender, politics and democracy in the Nordic countries entitled *Equal Democracies: Gender and Politics in the Nordic Countries*, Bergqvist et al. (1999) argue that it is possible to talk about a specifically Nordic gender model "as far as women's representation in the various parliaments is concerned" (ibid.: 278).

The percentage of women representatives in the national Parliaments and among Ministers are the highest in Scandinavia in the world context.

All the Scandinavian countries have developed and institutionalized equal status legislation which prohibits discrimination on the basis of sex, supplemented with a statutory requirement to take positive action in relation to equal status (Borchrost 1999). Gender equality legislation in the Scandinavian countries has primarily targeted the labour market and a key characteristic has been active use of quotas in the political field, especially in Norway and Sweden.[3] Quotas have been subject to intense discussions and disagreements. While opponents argue that quotas clash with the principle of selecting the best qualified applicant, advocates underline the fact that this is a necessary step to overcome institutionalized structural barriers that disadvantage especially women. Representation of women in politics and public committees increased in all countries following these measures, most notably in Norway and Sweden (Borchrost 1999).

Women's existence in politics made a difference and has been instrumental in bringing concerns that would otherwise be labelled "private" into the political agenda. The arguments related to gendered division of care work and housework and the difficulties of combining parenthood and employment moved to the centre of the political field.

Scandinavian Family Policies and Practices: The Private Becomes Political

A redrawing of boundaries between the public and the private spheres, mainly between the welfare state and the family is a key characteristic of the Scandinavian gender regime (Leira 2002). Through pervasive intervention into gender and family arrangements, the Scandinavian welfare states pioneered the transformation of parenthood into political issues:

> Politicising parenthood includes the public motivation and mobilization for reform of policies of parenthood; the political processes in which these policies are formulated, legislated and enacted; and finally, the public and parental response to policy interventions, that may in turn feed back into public debate and political mobilization, policy formulation and so on (Ellingsæter and Leira 2006a: 4).

Questions concerning the gendered division of paid and unpaid labour rank high on the political agenda. The model Nordic family is a dual-earner family. According to Skjeie and Siim (2000) two "grand inclusions" characterize Scandinavian

---

3   Borchorst et al. (1999) underline that gender equality policy agenda has been more restricted in Denmark than in the other Nordic countries.

Table 3.2   Labour force participation and fertility rates in selected countries

Country	Fertility rate (2005)	Women's (15-64 years old) employment rate (2006)
Iceland	2.0	82
Denmark	1.8	73
Norway	1.8	72
Sweden	1.7	72
Finland	1.8	67
Portugal	1.4	62
Spain	1.3	54
Italy	1.3	46
Greece	1.3	47

Source: OECD Factbook 2008.

citizenship: In terms of political citizenship, the dramatic increase in women's participation in decision-making bodies; and in terms of social citizenship, the move away from a male breadwinner to a dual breadwinner model (ibid.: 347). In the Scandinavian welfare states, work–family tensions arising from the erosion of the male breadwinner model have been modified by state policies (Ellingsæter 1999).

A more symmetric family model in which both the mother and the father are income-earners and carers can be supported by policy measures, such as full coverage in public child care and access to paid parental leave. Studies show that it is easier to use "family friendly" policies when they are formulated as a universal right for all parents (like parental leave), rather than those that demand individual negotiations with employers (Brandth and Kvande 2001, and see Chapter 5). Many studies document that the Nordic welfare states are the most supportive of the dual-earner family (e.g. Korpi 2000). The well institutionalized parental leave policies and publicly subsidized child care enabled Scandinavian mothers to enter and remain in the labour market (although often on a part-time basis).

In their analysis of the Nordic fertility patterns, Marit Rønsen and Kari Skrede (2006) argue that the Nordic welfare model has loosened the traditional negative link between a woman's employment and fertility by making childbearing more compatible with participation in the labour market (Rønsen and Skrede 2006: 62). Currently, Nordic fertility rates and mothers' employment rates rank among the highest in Europe.

Table 3.2 shows a north–south distinction with respect to fertility rates and women's employment patterns: Scandinavian countries display higher fertility rates combined with more women in the labour market, while Mediterranean countries display a combination of lower fertility rates with fewer women in the labour market. Esping-Andersen et al. (2001) point out a "trade-off" between employment and motherhood for Southern European women:

> Patterns of female labour supply are converging, but actual employment rates and fertility are not. In many countries, young women bear the lion's share of unemployment and/or of precarious employment. In Southern Europe, the trade-off between employment and motherhood is especially severe due to the lack of affordable childcare and of part-time jobs. The result is extremely low fertility (as in Spain and Italy) (Esping-Andersen et al. 2001: 83).

There is a critical relationship between women's employment patterns and fertility rates. In Sweden, the sharp decline in women's employment rates in the 1990s, due to economic recession, was followed by a fall in total fertility rate from 2.1 in 1990 to 1.5 in 1997 (Ellingsæter 2000b).

As Rønsen and Skrede (2006) underline, in order to understand fertility dynamics, we need to go beyond crude fertility rates and try to understand trends among different socioeconomic groups of women. Nevertheless it is generally accepted that the combination of high fertility and labour market participation is achieved through extensive public support for childcare combined with a focus on altering the gendered division of care by measures to increase fathers' participation in the care of their children.

Public Childcare and Parental Leave Policies in Scandinavia

Organized childcare outside the home has been a key demand of the women's movement of the 1970s (Bergqvist 1999). The planning, provision, funding and quality control of day care for preschool children was defined as a responsibility of the state and local government in the national legislation all the Nordic countries at the end of the 1970s (Leira 2006).

A general principle of public responsibility for child care prevails in Scandinavia. But there are differences between the countries with respect to organization of collective childcare. There have been important variations in coverage of childcare services. Danish policy has historically encouraged public childcare services for the youngest children (Ellingsæter 2000b). Analyses carried on in 1980s and 1990s reported Norway as the odd case since the percentage of young children (under 3s) attending publicly funded childcare was significantly lower than the other Scandinavian countries. This phenomenon will be analysed in detail in the case study at the end of this chapter.

A relatively long period of paid parental leave with high compensation rates is also an important element of Scandinavian gender model. Sweden was the first country to institutionalize paid parental leave by transforming the traditional maternity leave entitlements into leave rights for both parents in 1974. Norway followed in 1978 (Leira 2006). In this case, Denmark has been the laggard, having the shortest leave until early 2000s. Through the introduction of parental leave schemes, the feminist idea that "fathers as well as mothers can and should be responsible for the care of infants was legitimized through state regulation" (Bergqvist 1999b: 124).

As Bergqvist underlines, a policy of shared parental leave has a greater impact on the private sphere than a policy of institutionalized care, since it directly aims at altering the traditional gender-based division of labour:

> If fathers of small children were to use their entitlement to parental leave to the same extent as mothers, this would have major consequences for the organization of paid wok and the way in which gender is conceptualized. Another important notion has been that an entitlement to parental leave offers opportunities for both men and women to develop closer relations with their children that could generate positive effects for children, the family and society (Bergqvist 1999b: 125).

Even though it was revolutionary to institutionalize paid leave as a "choice" for fathers, their actual use of the leave has been merely symbolic throughout 1980s. Norway was the first country to introduce a forced father's quota in 1993, with Sweden following in 1995 and Denmark in 1998. Four weeks of the parental leave was reserved for the father and was not transferable to the mother. This "gentle force" resulted in a rapid increase in the percentage of fathers using parental leave: While only 2 per cent of Norwegian fathers took parental leave in 1992, 45 per cent "chose" to do so in 1994 (Brandth and Kvande 2003). The take-up continued to increase steadily, reached 80 per cent in 1998 and was 87 per cent in 2006. In 2006, the quota was also extended to 6 weeks (SSB nd).[4]

While Norway extended its paternity leave, Denmark went the opposite direction and abolished it in 2002. In her analysis of the abolishment of the Danish paternity leave, Borchorst (2006) argues that the caring role of the fathers has been subject to relatively weak politicization in Denmark, compared to the other Scandinavian countries (ibid.: 115). The abolishment also reminds us of the co-existence of different political trends and policy paradoxes in Scandinavia.

In *Working Parents and the Welfare State: Family Change and Policy Reform* in *Scandinavia* Leira (2002) identifies co-existing currents of both de-familialization and re-familialization in Scandinavia. While de-familialization refers to the public support of extra-family childcare, re-familialization refers to policy measures that support parental care for children at home (Leira 2002: 42). Leira argues that in the 1990s, childcare related policies in Finland, Norway and Sweden have promoted two

---

4   For more details on the use of fathers' quota in Norway, see the case study below.

different approaches to the combination of work and childcare. Although state support for families with young children is commonly accepted, there is wide disagreement over the form it should take: Cash transfers or provision of childcare services (ibid.: 142). Leira uses the term "state familism" referring to the policies targeting different models of the dual-parent family and argues that state familism comes in two forms in Scandinavia: One aims to support the male breadwinner-female carer family model (through cash benefit schemes) and the other aims to challenge the traditional family arrangement (through parental leave schemes for fathers). This point takes us to a brief discussion of the challenges facing the Scandinavian gender regime.

Pitfalls of the Scandinavian Gender Regime

The highly segregated labour market and few women at the top of the hierarchy are two factors often shown as a negative, unintended, consequence of the Scandinavian welfare model. Occupational segregation means that Scandinavian women and men do not compete for the same jobs, and men generally retain the high paying jobs. This is usually related to women's dominance in the public sector, which offers flexible, yet not very well paid, jobs.

Another pertinent problem has been the gendered division of housework which has been very slow to change. Yet, recent time-use studies show that Nordic men use more time for housework compared to their Southern counterparts, even though equity in gendered time-use is far from achieved (Rydenstam and Vaage 2008).

A serious challenge for the Scandinavian Model stems from an in-built element of the system, namely universalism. Universal entitlements are the basis of solidarity and a key mechanism of social inclusion and equality. Yet, this focus on egalitarianism brings the risk of and at the same time demands social homogeneity. In this context, one question presents itself as crucial to ask but hard to answer: How to deal with the tendency of "equality" claims becoming a demand for "sameness?" (cf. Gullestad 1992).

In her arguments in favour of the Scandinavian model, Hernes (1987) had underlined that egalitarian values and practices have had a positive effect on the welfare of women, but they have limitations when it comes to introducing pluralism in any form. One of the current discussions within Scandinavia is related to the challenges of cultural diversity and a growing need to focus on the intersections of gender, ethnicity and class (e.g. Williams 2008).

Another challenge for the Scandinavian gender regime is the danger of exhaustion and indifference resulting from a long history of focusing on gender equality. Many studies show that younger generations are taking gender equality for granted and some even think that equality has gone too far. For example,

Ellingsæter and Leira (2006b) argue that gender equality as a policy issue is loosing ground:

> The paradoxical reason for this may be that gender equality values are taken for granted, or alternatively that gender equality is considered as having gone too far, while pluralization, individualization and free choice are gaining ground ideologically and in practice (ibid.: 274).

Ellingsæter and Leira (ibid.: 275) state that under the redesign of the Scandinavian welfare states questions about individual responsibility and the limits of solidarity are emerging and "gender equality of outcomes" is fading out as one of the central policy aims.

Basing her arguments on recent studies on the Nordic model, Ruth Lister (2006) summarizes the remaining challenges and inconsistencies in Scandinavian countries underlining the gender segregations in the labour market and in the gendered division of care work. She adds another important point referring to the challenges to the women-friendly Nordic model created by immigration and multi-culturalism (Lister 2006). Many Scandinavian feminist social scientists also mentioned this factor as an important challenge for the Nordic model and argued for new forms of gender solidarity that is able to embrace women of different ethnic and religious backgrounds (e.g. Borchorst and Siim 2002; Siim 2000).

As elsewhere in Europe, Scandinavian women are divided by social class, age and ethnicity. The recent policy transformations are often conceived as mainly benefiting women with higher education in middle class occupations. The discussions concerning diversity and the challenge of integrating women of different ethnic and religious backgrounds remain as key issues on the agenda (Lister 2006).

A detailed analysis of the developments of gender equality and family policies in Norway may provide deeper insight into the challenges faced by the Scandinavian welfare model together with the idiosyncratic paradoxes of the Norwegian case.

Norway: An Odd Case in Scandinavia?

In 1980s and early 1990s, Norway was depicted as the odd case in Scandinavia due to lacking public responsibility for care of the youngest children and comprehensive support for women in their traditional roles as mothers and caregivers (e.g. Leira 1989; Sainsbury 1994). Starting from 1990s, important reforms took place to support mothers' employment. However, ambiguities continued to prevail leading to the characterization of Norway as a "hybrid" case (Ellingsæter 2003). Norway has also been characterized as "laggard" in the Scandinavian context with respect to later entrance of married women in paid employment. This factor is often explained referring to Norway's later urbanization, differences in party alliances and women's mobilization patterns (Knudsen and Wærness 2001, Sainsbury 1999, Skrede 2002). The detailed case study in this section is designed to throw a light on these peculiarities of the Norwegian case.

Compared to its Scandinavian neighbours, Norway has been a late-comer in industrialization. The absence of an aristocracy and the large number of independent peasants combined to make Norway an unusually egalitarian country (Esping-Andersen 1985: 46). A remarkable feature of Norwegian politics is the extent to which the bourgeois parties incorporated social democratic programs. Traditional left/right divisions have been weakened in the Norwegian parliament and most welfare reforms are achieved through party alliances and compromises. The North Sea oil revenues enabled Norway to sustain full employment and maintain welfare state expansion throughout the 1990s. Nonetheless, a neo-liberal orientation has become more visible in recent years, with a stronger emphasis on incentives to work and debates on the alleged detrimental effects of a comprehensive welfare state (Eitrheim and Kuhnle 2000). Yet, it will not be wrong to claim that social homogeneity and strong egalitarian traditions continue to be distinctive characteristics of contemporary Norwegian society. The 2000s so far have been characterized by continuing political consensus about the public responsibility for welfare provision, although privatization of certain welfare services and the so-called modernization of the public sector are key themes on the political agenda (Nilsen et al. 2004).

Norwegians often express pride when their country ranks as number one year after year according to the gender equality index of the United Nations. Many newspapers carry this to their front page and declare that Norway is the best place to live for women. In order to understand the bases of the current gender equality practices and institutions in Norway, a brief historical account is useful.

In the past, the division of labour in the Norwegian farms was one where the wife tended the farm while the husband went fishing or hunting. Women were thus often used to rough work and to being alone for long periods with major responsibility for the farm and the household (Gullestad 1992). This historical division of labour, together with the prevalence of the social democratic ideal of equality, have been important factors in shaping women's status in the Norwegian society.

The Norwegian Women's Movement Association was founded in 1884 and it had a strong pioneering influence on women's liberation movement, which became influential in the society throughout the 1970s (Haavio-Mannila 1981). Norway has developed rather strong instruments for the promotion of gender equality. Throughout the 1980s, reforms in family policies have gone hand in hand with the increased participation of women in the labour market and with the emphasis on the need to reconcile working life with family responsibilities for both parents.

Legislation and Machinery[5]

The Gender Equality Act, which was put into practice in 1979, prohibits discrimination based on gender in all areas of society, except for internal matters in religious communities. The Act permits positive differential treatment in order to promote gender equality, particularly to advance the position of women. The Act came into force in 1979, and has subsequently been amended several times, most recently in 2005 (CEDAW report 2006):

> The reason for the amendments was to ensure the satisfactory implementation of Directive...of the European Parliament and of the Council (on the implementation of the principle of equal treatment for men and women as regards access to employment, vocational training and promotion, and working conditions), the purpose of which was to strengthen gender equality. The legislative amendments were also made in order to ensure the harmonization of the Gender Equality Act and the Working Environment Act and the Act on prohibition of discrimination based on ethnicity, religion, etc. (the Anti-Discrimination Act). All these statutes have been enforced by a common enforcement machinery since 1 January 2006 (CEDAW 2006).

Throughout the 1990s, the Ministry of Children and Family Affairs had the coordinating and initiating responsibility for gender equality. On 1 January 2006, it changed name and became the Ministry of Children and Equality. Until the end of 2005, the Gender Equality Act was enforced by the Gender Equality Ombud and the Gender Equality Board of Appeals. As of 1 January 2006, this responsibility was transferred to the new Equality and Anti-Discrimination Ombud and the Equality and Anti-Discrimination Tribunal, which also enforce prohibition of discrimination based on other grounds. These are central government bodies that are professionally independent that deal with complaints free of charge (CEDAW 2006).

The official report of Norway to UN explains the reason of these changes in the following way:

> The reason for establishing a common machinery was to strengthen efforts to prevent discrimination and promote equality by adopting a greater interdisciplinary approach, make more effective use of resources and achieve

5   Parts of this section rely on Norway's seventh periodic report to the United Nations on Norway's implementation of the United Nations Convention on the Elimination of All Forms of Discrimination against Women referred to as CEDAW 2006.

greater impact and visibility than can be achieved with agencies as small and discrete as those currently operating in this field (CEDAW 2006: 7).

The Gender Equality Act requires public authorities to make systematic, targeted efforts to promote equality between women and men in all areas of society. To fulfil this obligation of active commitment, Norway has pursued the policy of gender mainstreaming, i.e. integrating a gender and equality perspective into all areas of policy in central government administration since the mid-1980s.

All ministries are expected to integrate a gender perspective and the goal of gender equality in policy formulation, decision-making and executive procedures at all levels and in all policy areas:

> The strategy of gender mainstreaming in order to implement Norwegian gender equality policies involves a proactive intervention in the policy processes to prevent gender inequalities. This is a way to integrate equal opportunities principles, strategies and practices into the every day work of government and other public authorities in Norway (Gender in Norway nd).[6]

Norway uses gender mainstreaming as an overall strategy for gender equality, but keeps gender specific action as an equally important approach. The Beijing Platform for Action (from the 4th UN Conference on Women in Beijing in 1995) called upon the UN member states to promote gender equality through the use of a dual strategy, namely to complement gender mainstreaming by policies targeted to address specific challenges.

Gender specific measures are widely employed in Norway, especially in the labour market and education. For example, as of 1 January 2004, the boards in all state owned companies are obliged to have a minimum of 40 per cent representation of each gender. The Parliament has passed corresponding amendments regarding public limited companies in the private sector. This has been regarded as a revolutionary step making Norway the first country in the world demanding gender balance within the boards of public limited companies (Ministry of Children and Equality).

The official website "Gender in Norway" underscores that the positive discrimination measures have caused a great deal of debate in Norway, but despite controversies Norway is probably one of the countries in the world that employs the most radical measures. The importance of the dual track strategy is underlined:

---

6   *Gender in Norway* (http://gender.no) is an English language information service about official gender equality work, gender research, and gender statistics in Norway. It is the result of a collaboration between various public agencies in Norway.

The strategy of positive measures cannot be used alone; it has to go hand in hand with the strategy of gender mainstreaming. Focusing exclusively on specific measures makes gender equality solely a women's issue. Previous strategies have looked on women as needing special attention, but the gender mainstreaming strategy makes men change too, because it focuses on transforming systems (Gender in Norway nd).

Norway's main strategy in achieving gender equality has been to strengthen women's economic independence through increasing their labour market participation. Another key focus has been political participation. The next section will provide brief information on the Norwegian women's participation patterns in politics, education and the labour market.

Norwegian Women in Politics

Political participation is crucial for gaining power to make a difference in the way state policies address gender. Norwegian women achieved full suffrage in 1913, but many years had to pass before women were elected to political bodies in favourable numbers. In 1945 only 4.7 per cent of the Parliament members were women, while in 1994 this percentage raised to a record high of 38. Following a brief fall in 1997 and 2001 elections, the percentage of female members in the Parliament rose to 38 per cent again in 2005 (SSB).[7]

Currently, the representation levels of Norwegian women in politics compare favourably with world averages. Only Sweden has a higher representation of women in the national Parliament.

Campaigns and gender quotas have been the most effective means to increase the proportion of women in the decision-making processes. Quotas have proved the most effective means of achieving a more equal balance of women and men in political bodies. Four of the six major Norwegian parties apply a gender quota system in nominations for elections and in the composition of committees at all levels. The goal of 40 per cent women in parliament and the Government, as well as in county councils, has been achieved. The proportion of women in municipal councils also rose sharply throughout the 1990s and was 36 per cent in 2003 and 37.5 per cent after the 2007 local elections (SSB).

---

7   Most of the statistics in this section are from the internet pages of Statistics Norway (referred to as SSB) which is the official organization responsible for providing statistics on a wide range of topics available online at: http://www.ssb.no

Norwegian Women in Education

Education level of the Norwegian women increased steadily throughout the 1980s and since the mid 1980s women have been majority among students of higher education. In 2007, women attained 65 per cent of the undergraduate degrees and 64 per cent of the graduate degrees at the universities. The same year women made up 44.5 per cent of the PhD graduates but only 18 per cent of the professors in the university sector (Women in Science).[8]

As the CEDAW reports underscore, choices made at the upper secondary level has a major impact on the students' educational path:

> Norwegian women and men tend to choose traditional educational and career paths. The gender balance is most equitable in upper secondary education, but it declines in step with the level of education. Men are dominant in technical and science subjects, while women are in the majority in teacher training, education, and health and social subjects (CEDAW 2006: 43).

Statistics show that in many subjects student choices are conservative. Influencing the occupational preferences of men and women in order to create a less gender-segregated labour market is an ongoing challenge. There are few women studying, for example natural science, mathematics and information technology. Positive measures have been taken in many technical colleges in order to increase the proportion of women in science and technology but the progress in this field is slow. 91 per cent of students who chose health and social studies in the upper secondary schools were females, while only 5 per cent chose technical studies. There are clear gendered patterns in certain fields of higher education as well (see Table 3.3). Norway's official CEDAW report discusses the relation between educational choices and wage differentials between men and women as a key challenge:

Table 3.3   Gender distribution of students in selected higher education programs in Norway (per cent rounded), 2003

Subject	Women	Men
Preschool teaching	92	8
Nursing	89	11
Engineering	17	83

Source: Gender in Norway.

---

8   Women in science is an online information source for those who work to improve the gender balance in the research sector: http://kvinneriforskning.no/english/

As a result of their educational choices, a majority of women end up in less well paid jobs than men. In terms of untraditional career choices, more women than men choose untraditional careers because they have more to gain financially. Men will probably continue to be in the minority in occupations where there is a need for more equitable distribution of women and men, such as nursing, teaching and pre-school teaching. Until the female-dominated professions are paid at the same level as the male-dominated professions it will be difficult to challenge the gender-segregated labour market. The goal of more equal gender distribution presents a challenge for the social partners in wage negotiations (CEDAW 2006: 43).

Norwegian Women in the Labour Market

The labour market is an important arena for efforts to promote gender equality and to improve the position of women. Norwegian working environment legislation contains strict requirements to ensure that both female and male workers have good rights in connection with pregnancy, birth and child care (CEDAW 2006).

Labour force participation for women increased significantly from the beginning of the 1970s until the end of the 1980s but remained more or less stable for men. During the economic recession from the end of the 1980s to 1993, the participation rate for women remained steady, but fell for men. Subsequently, numbers have increased for both sexes. In 2004, the labour force was made up of 69 per cent of women and 76 per cent of men aged 16-74 (SSB nd).

The welfare state has been characterized as an "employment machine" for women (Wærness 1998). The greatest labour market for women is the welfare state services in health, care and education. In 2006, 47 per cent of women and 19 per cent of men worked in the public sector (SSB nd). These figures have remained stable over the last few years. Women are more often employed in the local government sector. Typical female professions are teachers in kindergartens, primary and secondary schools, nurses and secretaries (SSB 2006).

Despite the convergence in the employment figures for women and men, there are still major differences in terms of working hours, pay, sectors and pensions. There are still far more women than men in part-time employment. However, there are fewer women and more men working part-time today than ten years ago. In 1990, 48 per cent of women worked part-time (compared with 9 per cent of men) in 2006, the figure was 42 per cent (compared with 12 per cent of men). Women with more than one child under the age of 16 are the most likely to work part-time. For men, part-time work is more common as a supplement to studies or towards the end of their working life (CEDAW 2006).

The Norwegian labour market is strongly divided between the sexes (Solheim and Ellingstaeter). A majority of women are employed in sectors that retain lower salaries. When the differences in working hours and occupations are taken into account, women still earn only 87 per cent of men's salaries (SSB 2006). The discrepancy between women's and men's salaries is largest in the financial services industry (banking and insurance) where women earn only 74 per cent of men's salaries. The gap is smallest among teachers (SSB 2006).

In addition to this horizontal segregation, there is also a vertical segregation: Women have fewer chances than men of obtaining a high position within the occupational hierarchy. Women are still not very well represented at top management, though there have been important developments in this field in the last decade. In 1992, less than 10 per cent of senior management positions were held by women. In 2006 this percentage was 24. In the private sector 25 per cent of all managers are women. The corresponding ratio is 45 in the public sector (SSB nd). In the private sector as a whole, 22 per cent of the senior management posts and 17 per cent of CEOs were women in 2005.

Scarcity of women at the higher levels of the hierarchy has been a major research focus in Norway (for a review see Sümer and Nilsen 2004; Storvik 2002). Some have found that the image of the ideal leader that prevails in organizations is a masculine one, while other studies document that the ideals include both masculine and feminine traits. Some studies focus on women's own priorities and motivation, while others stress their care responsibilities and remaining traditional care arrangements (Sümer and Nilsen 2004).

Encouraging a more equal sharing of income producing and family work among mothers and fathers has been a major aim of the family policies in Norway. Gender equality policies are tightly related to family policies since a major aim of the welfare state is to promote a change in the traditional gender roles within the families.

Family Policies to Promote Equal Opportunities

There is a close link between family policies and gender equality policies. In the 1970s and 1980s, Norwegian family policies tended to provide support for women in their traditional roles as full-time housewives (Wærness 1999). Legislation on childcare services has been politically controversial since the 1970s, although access to high quality day-care for children over the age of three has generally been regarded as educationally advantageous (Knudsen and Wærness 2001). In contrast to the rest of Scandinavia, the large-scale investment in public childcare in Norway came too late to support mothers' entrance into the labour market. However, starting in the early 1990s, important reforms took place with the general purpose of enabling *both* parents to combine employment and parenthood responsibilities. Main objectives of the current family policies in Norway can be specified as:

- Facilitating more flexible arrangements between work and family for both mothers and fathers,
- Ensuring more freedom of choice between various childcare arrangements,
- Enabling parents to spend more time with their children,
- Encouraging a more equal sharing of income producing and family work among mothers and fathers (Kitterød and Kjeldstad 2002).

The period of paid parental leave was gradually extended throughout the 1980s and in 1993 was set at 42 weeks with full pay, or 52 weeks on an 80 per cent wage. Entitlement to parental benefits is earned through paid employment of minimum 6 months prior to birth. Women who do not qualify for parental leave receive a lump sum grant which was around €4,000 in 2000. Three weeks before and six weeks after birth are reserved as mother quota. A father quota—Four weeks' paid leave which cannot be transferred to the mother—was introduced in 1993. This was extended to six weeks in 2006. This extension is implemented by lengthening the total benefit period, which has been set to 44 weeks with full pay (and 54 weeks with 80 per cent compensation).

Parents of small children are entitled to reduce their working hours by law: "Both parents are entitled to work shorter hours if this is necessary for strong welfare reasons, such as the desire and need of parents of small children to spend more time with their children."[9]

In 2005 fathers' parental leave rights were strengthened in that the father's income compensation is no longer reduced if the mother works part-time prior to the birth. Previously the father was paid on the basis of the mother's fraction of a full-time post in such cases (CEDAW 2006: 67).

Though fathers had the opportunity to share paid leave with mothers earlier, only 2 per cent of them took advantage of it. After the introduction of this quota, which cannot be transferred to the mother, the percentage of fathers taking leave increased to over 85 per cent. Studies show that the likelihood that a father will use the quota increases when the mother works full-time and earns a relatively high income (Lappegård 2003). Father's quota is taken by around 87 per cent of fathers who are entitled to such leave. However, almost 40 per cent are not entitled, which means that in total only around 50 per cent of fathers take paternal leave. Fathers take 23 days leave on average, and this figure has been stable since 1994 (SSB nd).

---

9   A comprehensive brochure on the rights of the parents of small children in Norway is available online at: http://www.regjeringen.no/en/dep/bld/Documents/Guidelines-and-brochures/2007/The-rights-of-parents-of-small-children.html?id=454913

Table 3.4   **Changes in time use for Norwegian men and women (time use in hours and minutes in an average day)**

		1971	1990	2000
Women				
	Paid Work	1.53	3.11	3.39
	Housework	6.48	5.00	4.21
Men				
	Paid Work	6.03	5.19	5.37
	Housework	2.22	2.44	2.48

The time-use of mothers and fathers and the gendered division of family work is analyzed by time use surveys in Norway. These surveys show that in the last decades women have decreased the time they use for housework and markedly increased the time they use for wage-earning; while men decreased slightly the time they use for wage-earning and only slightly increased their share of housework (see Table 3.4).

An analysis of working time among couples with small children documents the differences between families with respect to education levels: Parents use a total of 73 hours at work when the mother has university education, as against a total of approximately 61 hours when the mother has only upper secondary education (Kitterød 2005).

In 1998, a cash-for-care policy was introduced. This policy implies that parents can choose a cash benefit instead of a day-care centre if they want to take care of their children themselves. The arrangement entitles all parents who have children between 1 and 3 years of age, who do not use state sponsored childcare, the same amount of money as the state subsidy per child (c. €375 per month). This "cash for home care" policy has been widely debated both among politicians and academics. It was a hot topic among feminist scholars at the end of the 1990s (e.g. Wærness 1998, Leira 1998). Various evaluations of the reform documented that cash-for-care policy did not have highly significant effects, neither on the work and time-use patterns of parents, nor on the implementation and demand for state-subsidized day care centres (Ellingsæter 2003, Knudsen and Wærness 2001).

Childcare policies have been controversial in Norway. The official childcare policy has been declared as providing full coverage in state subsidized day-care centres however there is a historical legacy of a lack of political consensus on the issue of public childcare (Ellingsæter 1999). Day-care institutions for children over 3 years of age have traditionally been more widely accepted than for those under 3. However, the supply for day-care places for youngest children still do not meet the demand and is a basic problem for parents of small children who want to combine parenthood and employment (Sümer et al. 2005).

Costs of the child care services are shared between the state, the municipality and the parents. In Norwegian society, at least among middle-class families, it is widely accepted that attending state subsidized day-care institutions is a positive contributor to the psychological and social development of children (Wærness 1998). Percentage of children in the age group 1-5 attending to a day-care has increased from 19 in 1980 to 69 in 2003 (SSB).

In 2004 national day care coverage for the 1-5 age group was 72 per cent. For the 3-5 age group the coverage rate was 88 per cent. Day care is now available for most of the parents who want a place for a child over the age of 3. For children under the age of 3, however, there are waiting lists in many parts of the country. At the end of 2004, 52 per cent of day care centres in Norway were privately owned. Yet, all kindergartens in Norway are centrally controlled by the local governments. The percentage of private day care centres has increased significantly in recent years and in 2004 a maximum limit for parents' payments was introduced (SSB).

Fertility Patterns

The dominant trend in Norwegian society is to delay births. The average age at first birth increased from 25 in 1987 to 28 in 2004 (SSB). Education level has an influence on postponement of childbirth. For the 1967 birth cohort, the median age at first birth was 21.9 for the group with lowest education while it was 30.7 for the group with highest education (a total education of 17-20 years) (Rønsen 2001).

The percentage of mothers with pre-school children who are in the labour market increased steadily since the 1970s. The labour force participation of mothers with children under the age of 6 increased to all time high in 2001: 86 per cent of mothers with a child between the ages of 3-6 were employed. This percentage has declined slightly in the following years. In 2003, 72 per cent of mothers with a child below the age of 3 and 80 per cent of mothers with a child between 3-6 years were participating in the labour market. Around 75 per cent of all Norwegian women are entitled to paid maternity leave. This number increases to almost 90 per cent for women with higher education (Danielsen and Lappegård 2003).

The studies on the connection between field of education and fertility show that women educated towards female-dominated occupations (mainly nurses and teachers) have more children than other groups of women. However, there is also a high fertility among women whose education has a high career orientation (e.g. doctors and dentists). In her study on the connection between field of education and fertility, Lappegård (2002) concludes that due to the existence of generous family benefits in Norway, a combination of work-career and childcare is possible in all parts of the labour market, and that there are relatively small variations in how many children women in different education groups will have.

Social class and educational level continue to create crucial divisions in Norwegian women's interests and preferences with regard to family and employment (Wærness 1998). However, a general preference for childcare institutions (especially for children over 3) remains a clear trait. Norwegians in general conceive defamilializing policies as positive and have high expectations concerning public support for their family-related problems. The expectations directed at the welfare state become even clearer when compared to countries that have different state and gender policy traditions (Sümer 2004). As I briefly mentioned in Chapter 1, my doctorate project was a comparative study of gender relations and family practices in urban Turkey and Norway based on complementary analyses of official documents, statistics and face-to-face interviews with Turkish and Norwegian dual-earner couples. This comparison revealed the general characteristics of the Scandinavian welfare model reflected in the Norwegian society. In concluding this case study of Norway, I will briefly present some of the findings pertaining individuals' conceptualization of and expectations from the welfare state in these two contrasting contexts.

Dual-earner Couples and the Welfare State[10]

As in other Scandinavian countries, the state is conceived as part of the Norwegian "community" and state interference in the family is interpreted as essentially positive. Most Norwegian women agree that the "transition from private to public dependency" (Hernes 1987) has primarily been beneficial. In my comparative analysis Norwegians had much higher and varied expectations, while many Turkish respondents had little to say concerning what they expect from the state.

Norwegian interviewees were mainly positive when they talked about the welfare state and they appreciated having a system that provides a basic "security network:"

> In a way, you expect that, if you fall out of the system in one way or another, you will be picked up again (38-year-old man).

Turkish interviewees, on the other hand, were critical about the present condition of the state and were pessimistic about the possibility of change. State assistance

---

10   This section draws on different chapters of my doctoral dissertation with the title *Global Issues/Local Troubles: A Comparative Study of Turkish and Norwegian Urban Dual-Earner Couples* (Sümer 2002). The quotations are excerpts from face-to-face interviews with dual-earner couples.

was generally conceived of as relevant only for those employed in the public sector or those who are in poverty. Opting for private alternatives, especially in the areas of education and health, was prevalent among Turkish dual-career couples.

In terms of family policies directed at dual-earner families, Turkey and Norway differed considerably. In Turkey, family is still conceptualized as predominantly "private" and the state is supposed to step in only as a last resort in cases of extreme poverty or violence. As the review above made clear, Norwegian family policies are comprehensive and are closely related to gender equality policies aiming at transforming the traditional gendered division of labour. Norwegian interviewees conceived state interference in family as essentially positive and had well-defined expectations. Many mentioned the benefits of having institutionalized arrangements which do not demand efforts from individuals:

> Maternity leave is very nice. Having the opportunity to be at home one year is after all a big benefit. And it is very well established; it functions well, that you have a child and you get the money without doing much about it (35-year-old woman)

One often cited disappointment was related to the scarcity of places in daycare and the relatively high costs:

> There are many good (childcare) arrangements...but they do not have full coverage in daycare centers, for example, and that is negative...And even though I am very fond of the daycare center, and think that it is worth every penny we pay, it is still quite expensive...(36-year-old man)

The institutional characteristics of the welfare system in Norway that result in a high sense of entitlement for public support and high expectations directed at social policy become evident when compared to a context characterized by a marginal and familialistic welfare state as in Turkey. The Norwegian example shows that the welfare state is capable of designing policies that are felt as "friendly" by different segments of the population (Sümer 2004). A well developed machinery and legal back-up is vital in promoting gender equality in different arenas of social life. This will also become apparent in the three country comparison that will be presented in Chapter 5.

Conclusions

The review of major policies and an account of how these policies have influenced gender relations in Scandinavia show that there have been important developments towards gender equality in the public sphere and a slow progress towards a fairer division of unpaid work in the private sphere. Our analysis also highlighted areas that are characterized by persistent segregations and stubborn gendered patterns.

Referring to the strongly gender-segregated labour markets and high levels of part-time employment for women, leading to important differences between mothers' and fathers' working time, Skrede (2004) characterizes the Scandinavian context as "gender equality light." This is an insider's evaluation of the Nordic model. Yet, the accomplishments tend to look as greater than the pitfalls when approached with a wider European perspective.

The favourable representation rates of women in politics mark the existence of a Nordic model. As Borchorst et al. (1999) stress in the conclusion of their in-depth study of gender and politics in Scandinavia, the processes of institutionalization are central in promotion of gender equality. Women's existence in politics makes a difference both for the development of political institutions and for the transformation of the political agenda.

Family policies that aim at supporting mothers' labour market participation and changing the traditional arrangements for childcare have in general been successful. The gender gap in employment rates and earnings has decreased. The percentage of fathers taking paid parental leave is not insignificant and there are studies documenting that many Norwegian men wish for an extension of their fatherhood rights (Pettersen 2003).

The persistent combination of relatively high fertility rates with high labour force participation of mothers in the past years led to a renewed interest in the Scandinavian gender regime. Many observers mentioned the "demographic time bomb" elsewhere in Europe and the option of turning to the Nordic model for possible solutions (Duncan 2002). The developments in the gender policies of the EU are significantly inspired by the Scandinavian model. This is what we turn to in the next chapter.

Chapter 4
Gender Policies in the European Union

The European Union (EU) is a grand project involving both economic and social ambitions. The relationship between the economic and social concerns and the difficult balancing act of the efficiency and equality concerns are widely discussed and there are contrasting views on the capability of the Union to promote social inclusion and cohesion. The "social dimension" of the European Union is a contested topic (for a detailed discussion see e.g. Hantrais 1995; Kleinman 2002). This chapter will explore the gender equality elements of the social policy agenda of the EU. A key purpose is to understand the dynamics of the developments of gender policies with a historical perspective. Another objective, which will be developed further in the next chapter, is an attempt to study how these supranational policies are influencing different local contexts.

The following review is guided by a question that is similar to the one posed by Mahon (2002: 361): "What design for community living informs the drive to establish a social Europe and what are the gender dimensions of this?" The focus will be on a critical assessment of the two key policy areas, namely work–family reconciliation and gender mainstreaming. The chapter will end with a discussion of different feminist views on the uses and abuses of EU policy.

Historical Development of Gender Policies in the EU

The idea of the European Union has developed in the restructuring period of the post-war Europe. The European Economic Community was established by the Treaty of Rome (1957) to maintain peace in Europe and to foster prosperity through cooperation. In 1968, all internal tariffs had been abolished among the Member States for a community wide production and distribution of products and services (Cotter 2004). The Maastricht Treaty (1992) created the European Union (EU) confirming its attachment to "the principles of liberty, democracy and respect for human rights and fundamental freedoms and of the rule of law" (Cotter 2004: 245).

On paper, the principle of gender equality is firmly integrated in the EU legislation. Article 2 of the European Community Treaty provides that promotion of equality between men and women is a task of the Community. The following quote from the communication from the European Commission (EC) on gender equality lays bare the critical relationship between the aims of economic growth and social cohesion:

> Gender equality is a fundamental right, a common value of the EU, and a necessary condition for the achievement of the EU objectives of growth, employment and social cohesion. The EU has made significant progress in achieving gender equality thanks to equal treatment legislation, gender mainstreaming, specific measures for the advancement of women, action programmes, social dialogue and dialogue with civil society (EC 2006: 2).

This passage summarizes the current approach that the Union has to the question of gender equality: It is specified as a key value, but at the same time it is depicted as instrumental in achieving economic growth. An historical analysis is indispensable to get an insight on this issue.

There has been a significant conceptual shift in European legislation concerning gender policy, from a focus on equal pay, to the "mainstreaming" approach. Scrutiny of European legislation confirms the conceptual shift from "women's policy"—in the sense of measures designed to bring women into line with men as workers—to "gender policy"—aimed at confronting socially constructed inequalities both at work and in the home (Hantrais 2000: 2).

The following definition of equality marks the evolution from sole economic concerns to a focus on changing the gender contract:

> The promotion of equality must not be confused with the simple objective of balancing the statistics: It is a question of promoting long-lasting changes in parental roles, family structures, institutional practices, the organization of work and time, personal development and independence; concerns not only women, but also men and the whole society (EC 1996).

Gender policies have expanded to tackle different barriers to women's equal opportunities, from childcare and parental leave, to harassment at work and the reversal of the burden of proof of discrimination from employees to employers (Hantrais 2000).

The origins of gender policy in the EU lie in Article 119 of the Treaty of Rome which guarantees the principle of equal pay for equal work regardless of sex. A typical characteristic of the early EU policies is a focus on equality only as it pertains to employment and a domination of economic considerations over social concerns. According to Ellina (2003) fear of imbalanced competition was the main reason behind the inclusion of gender equality in the Treaty. The intention was to create fair and equal competition between member states by preventing any one country from gaining a competitive edge by paying women at lower rates than men (Hantrais 2000). Still, many argue that Article 119 has a great significance since it provided both the policy makers and the women's lobby with a necessary "juridical hook on which to hang their demands" for further equality legislation (Mazey 1998: 138).

As primary legislation, treaties offer a source and a justification for the developments of secondary legislation, such as Directives. The gender policies of the EU developed mainly by means of "soft," legally non-binding policy instruments, such as action programmes and recommendations (Mazey 1998).

In an analysis of the four Action Programmes on equal opportunities, Catherine Hoskyns (2000) traces changing ideas and priorities in the EU from early 1980s up to 2000. The use of action programmes is standard practice in the EU for managing particular policy areas:

> Once the action programme is adopted, and the budget agreed upon, the precise aims and objectives set out in the text will provide the basis as appropriate for legislative proposals, the funding of projects, and the commissioning of studies and research (Hoskyns 2000, 45).

The first Action Programme (1982-85) was drawn up following a period of intense activism among women across Europe and it placed great emphasis on legal instruments for equal opportunities. In this period women's policy was established on a firmer base and its scope was expanded (Hoskyns 2000). The second Action Programme was drawn up in a context of prolonged recession and unemployment leading to a general inclination for deregulation and cost cutting across Europe. In this context, adopting new legislation in the social policy area was becoming increasingly difficult (ibid.: 48). The second Action Programme (1986-1990) developed a "multi-faceted" policy and emphasized a broad range of actions, including sharing of family and occupational responsibilities. The third Programme (1991-1995) included a new section on improving the status of women in society. This moved the policy away from a sole focus on employment to deal with the world of politics and the distribution of resources (ibid.: 50). The section also included the first discussion of "gender mainstreaming." The fourth action programme for equal opportunities (1996-2000) adopted gender mainstreaming as its main objective and became the vehicle for its promotion (Stratigaki 2005). This concept will be analysed in further detail later in this chapter.

Ellina (2003) provides a historical analysis of the EU legislation and characterizes 1990s as a period of intense policy development and a gradual expansion of EU gender policy to include non-market related issues. In 1991 a Recommendation on Sexual Harassment was issued, defining it as sex discrimination that limits women's labour force participation and in 1992 the Recommendation on Childcare was adopted.

This Recommendation proposes that initiatives are needed in four areas: Childcare services, leave for employed parents, to make the workplace responsive to the needs of workers with children and measures to promote increased participation by men in the care and upbringing of children (Moss 1996: 25).

The only binding policy came in 1992—the Directive on safety and health at work of pregnant workers, workers who have recently given birth or are breastfeeding. According to Guerrina (2002) the 1992 Pregnant Worker Directive marked a significant shift in EU policy making in the field of equal opportunities:

> It provides a minimum standard for the *protection* of working mothers in the EU, thus improving the legal standing of women in the member states where maternity legislation was weak or altogether absent...On the negative side, however, it also serves to reinforce the division between formal and substantive equality. This further dichotomization of the principle of equality occurs because EU legislation establishes a framework for the *protection* of women workers, rather than addressing calls for the *promotion* of women's rights as mothers and citizens (Guerrina 2002, 56 emphases original).

In the 1994 White Paper on European Social Policy a subsection was devoted to "reconciling employment and family life" on the grounds that it was in the interests of society as a whole that working life and family life should be more "mutually reinforcing" (Hantrais 2000).

Admission of Sweden and Finland to the EU in 1995 had a positive influence concerning development of gender equality legislation. Ellina (2003) argues that the Scandinavian countries brought into the EU a longer experience and stronger tradition regarding gender equality policies and changed the framework for gender policy (ibid.: 50). Several researchers in the field argue that the increasing focus on gender equality, a change in the parental roles and support for childcare at the EU level has a connection with the membership of "Nordic" countries (Bergqvist and Jungar 2000; Duncan 2002).

Another important turning point in 1995 was the EU's participation in the UN Women's Conference in Beijing with one delegation representing the 15 member states.

The 1996 Parental Leave Directive was the first agreement reached through the Social Dialogue.[1] The Directive has two specific objectives: It strives to establish a socioeconomic framework that allows women to reconcile professional and domestic responsibilities and it seeks to redefine gendered divisions of care work

---

1 This policy-making structure involves the main representatives of labour and management in the process.

by encouraging greater male participation. The main achievement of the Directive is the provision of a parental leave of three months for each parent.

In the 1997 Amsterdam Treaty, two key articles on gender were introduced: Article 2 that includes equality between men and women as a Community task, on equal footing with economic convergence and employment promotion; and Article 3 that introduces a legal standing for the concept of mainstreaming.

Since the Amsterdam Treaty, equal opportunity has become one of the four columns of the labour market policies in the EU, alongside employability, adaptability, and entrepreneurship (von Wahl 2005: 84).

The Lisbon European Council 2000 identified a set of challenges for the "Social Policy Agenda." The aim of the new Social Policy Agenda is to strengthen the role of social policy as a productive factor, calling for new social policies to respond to changing work patterns, family structures and persistent gender inequalities. The approach identified in the agenda, which should be common across Europe is the promotion of quality. The promotion of better jobs is seen as a key element and better jobs do include more balanced ways of combining working and personal life (EC 2006).

There are two specific policy objectives set out in the Agenda concerning gender equality. The first one is to raise the proportion of women in work to 60 per cent in 2010 and the other is promoting gender equality, in particular by assisting in reconciliation of family and working life.

In 2002, the European Council acknowledged the importance of childcare in establishing equal opportunities and called on member states to provide childcare to at least 90 per cent of children between 3 years old and the mandatory school age and at least 33 per cent of children under 3 years of age by 2010—the so-called Barcelona targets.

The EU reaffirmed its commitment to gender equality in the social agenda 2005-2010, which complements the renewed Lisbon strategy for growth and jobs. Four priorities are specified: Addressing gender roles, promoting women in decision making, supporting work-life balance and tackling the gender pay gap (European Commission 2005).

The *Gender Equality Report* (2005) of the European Commission documented the persistent gender pay gap and showed that reconciling work and family life remained a problem for many women. Unbalanced division of domestic work and lack of affordable childcare are specified as serious obstacles to gender equality in the report. While obvious pay discrimination for identical work has been almost completely eliminated, the struggle for equal earnings per hour worked continues since vertical and horizontal segregation persists and what is labelled women's work remains undervalued.

As specified in a recent report (EC 2008) current EU gender policy is characterized by a continuing promotion of gender mainstreaming and a special emphasis on women's increasing participation in the labour market. "More and better jobs for women" is specified as first priority in the Commissions report on equality between men and women (EC 2008).

The *Roadmap For Equality Between Women and Men 2006-2010* prepared by the EC outlines six priority areas for action on gender equality:

1. equal economic independence for women and men
2. reconciliation of private and professional life
3. equal representation in decision-making
4. eradication of all forms of gender-based violence
5. elimination of gender stereotypes
6. promotion of gender equality in external and development policies (EC 2006a: 2)

The roadmap underlines that even though man women entered the labour market, inequalities remain and may widen "as increased global economic competition requires a more flexible and mobile labour force" (ibid.).

Different Feminist Views on EU Policies

Feminists are divided with respect to their general attitudes towards the EU and its gender policies. While some underline the importance of an alliance with the EU, especially in those countries with historically weak women's movements (e.g. Walby 2004) others dismiss it as basically a market-oriented project bound to increase social inequalities (e.g. Rossilli 2000, Young 2000).

It is important to underline a north–south divide with respect to perception and benefit of EU gender policies. The historically familialistic Mediterranean countries had to level up their parental leave schemes and adjust their equal opportunities legislation. Feminist researchers from Mediterranean countries tend to underline the positive contributions from the EU agenda (Sümer et al. 2008). Nordic feminists, on the other hand, have historically been more sceptical of the EU. Reviewing the situation in Sweden, Bergqvist and Jungar (2000) argue that even though Swedish women generally were more negative towards the EU project than men, with a fear of loosing their hard earned benefits, the EU membership did not lead to a negative development in this field so far.

Many observers underline the opportunities provided by the EU as a special supranational body in influencing local national contexts. For example, Mahon (2002) argues that "the thickening of a European discursive and legislative space opens up the possibility of injecting new ideas concerning gender equality into national regimes" (ibid.: 360).

> Embedding the universal caregiver model in European benchmarks and guidelines can contribute to the establishment of a new horizon of legitimate expectations, encouraging egalitarian forces in all member states and thus helping shift the balance in their favour (Mahon 2002: 366).

Another optimistic feminist voice, Sylvia Walby (2004, 2005), argues that EU has significant potential to have a positive impact on gender equality. Walby thinks that a wide range of inequalities may be addressed by the EU and that the gender regime developing in the EU has specific merits compared to the one developing in the US since the new variety of gender regime in the EU has a public form shaped by a distinctive institutionalized practice of social inclusion, articulated through employment-based set of regulations (Walby 2004: 23).

Many scholars point at the key problem of implementation of the policies on paper in various local contexts. For example, Roberta Guerrina argues that the Council Resolutions and Recommendations are all examples of soft law which is not legally binding and therefore lack the power to ensure the successful implementation of its objectives in member states (Guerrina 2002: 60). She also highlights that EU policies in the field of gender are not cohesive:

> On the one hand, the 1992 Pregnant Worker Directive highlights the persistence of formal equality as the primary objective of European law; on the other, the 1996 Parental Leave Directive entails a more critical assessment of gender roles and gendered divisions of labour. The question that needs to be addressed with reference to the future of EU policies in this field is as follows: To what extent will the Parental Leave Directive challenge the status quo and foster a more cohesive approach that will allow future policies to bridge the gap between formal and substantive equality? (Guerrina 2002: 58)

Critiques of the EU gender policy tend to underline the dominating neo-liberal orientation in which economic concerns overshadow the feminist ones. According to Jane Lewis (2006) gender equality is defined primarily in terms of labour market participation and EU's commitment to equality is predominantly understood as "same treatment according to the male mainstream model" (Lewis 2006: 433). Lewis et al. (2008) argue that the policy developments at the EU level appeared to be instrumental since they serve first and foremost the agendas of competition and growth rather than "family welfare, child well-being, parental choice or gender equality per se" (Lewis et al. 2008, 22).

Another feminist researcher who is basically critical to the EU, Ilona Ostner (2000), argues that EU social policies have been guided by regulation policies to remove market barriers. According to Ostner, EU policy logic displays a shift from decommodification to recommodification, abandoning redistribution that is needed for compensating those out of employment:

> In sum, equal opportunities have gained a new meaning as equality of employability of women and men (Ostner 2000, 39).

Mariagrazia Rossilli (2000) draws attention to the double sided effects of the EU policies, mentioning that on the one hand, they have contributed to creating new employment opportunities for women, but on the other hand, they have contributed to increasing gender inequalities in terms of occupational segregation, wage differential, and social benefits (Rosilli 2000: 10). Rosilli claims that European Community action has weakened women's social rights more seriously than men's:

> With the weakening of welfare systems and restriction of the social rights of citizens to the working population, the gender hierarchy implicitly embedded in the very notion of *worker* weighs more and more heavily on the social citizenship of women, especially of those from the weakest social strata (Rossilli 2000, 10).

Brigitte Young (2000) dismisses EU policy as "disciplinary neoliberalism" arguing that the development of equal opportunities policies fit into the pro-market-forming activities of the neoliberal governance structure and their feminist potential are severely limited. She asserts that equal opportunity policies facilitate the development of flexible labour markets by getting rid of unwanted protective regulations:

> The 'new gender contract' requires a new working time regime for both men and women enabling them to combine flexibly paid work and unpaid work...Women are thus in the process of finally reaching the long awaited abstract equality with men—not in terms of wages, but in respect of an abstract notion of individualism that is free at last from reproductive activities (Young 2000: 95).

Simon Duncan (2002), on the other hand, argues that we are faced with a "half-empty or half-full" problem in assessing the role of the EU. He mentions the work of Young (2000) briefly mentioned above as an example for the "half-empty" position. Duncan endorses a "half-full" view on EU gender policy, claiming that much of the negative critique stems from the 1980s situation. He argues that since then EU gender policy has been transformed to acknowledge the centrality of changing the traditional gender contract. This position conceives the EU as a powerful polity, which has the legal means to ensure that its ruling have considerable effect.

According to Duncan the EU focus on work–family reconciliation is basically positive and this offers a real means of generalizing from the Scandinavian gender equality model:

> True, the central EU debate is one of achieving economic success in a globalised, capitalist world, but within this gender equality has moved centre stage if only because 'reconciling work and life' is now seen as necessary for this success (Duncan 2002: 313).

This assertion takes us to a more detailed analysis of two major fields in the changing EU gender policy context. We will first review different views on the concept of work–family reconciliation and then summarize important feminist analyses of the concept of gender mainstreaming.

Reconciliation of Work and Family

Changes in family patterns and gender relations, together with women's increasing education and labour force participation rates are the key factors behind the need to formulate policies to support parents to combine their family and work obligations. The male-breadwinner/female carer (housewife) model, underpinning welfare policies of most European countries in the post-war area has been undermined by women's increasing labour market participation and family transformations (Pascall and Lewis 2004: 374). Falling fertility rates is another major concern for European governments.

Having no authority in family policy, the EU introduced the concept of reconciling work and family to facilitate equal opportunities for women in the labour market (Stratigaki 2004). The term "reconciliation" itself has been debated and found confusing. Reconciliation implies an attempt to harmonize different interests "so that they can be conducted with as little friction and stress as possible" (Moss 1996: 23). It implies a more interactional approach compared to the other often used concept of "family-friendly" since it accommodates the possibility of conflicts of interests:

> The term 'reconciliation' implies the need to seek accommodation between various needs and interests—of employers, but also children, other 'cared for' groups, women men and society—and as such indicates a more differentiated and interactional approach than 'family-friendly' (Moss 1996: 23).

The initial work on reconciliation issues goes back to 1970s. The 1974 Social Action Programme of the (then) European Community called for action "to ensure that the family responsibilities of all concerned may be reconciled with their job aspirations" (Moss 1996: 23).

However, the first piece of legislation came two decades later in 1994. In the White Paper on European Social Policy a subsection was devoted to "reconciling employment and family life" on the grounds that it was in the interests of society as a whole that working life and family life should be more "mutually reinforcing." Two key issues were explicitly addressed:

- How to manage and support the relationship between working time and time spent caring for children and older people.
- How to encourage more effective sharing of responsibilities for care between men and women (Hantrais 2000).

The binding legislation in this field came with the 1996 Parental Leave Directive. It had two specific objectives: Establishing a socioeconomic framework that will allow women to reconcile professional and domestic responsibilities and redefining gendered divisions of labour in the practice of care by encouraging greater male participation in domestic responsibilities (Guerrina 2002).The chief accomplishment of this Directive was the provision of a minimum right to parental leave of three months for each parent.

Duncan (2002) argues that the policy focus on reconciliation was a critical "tip-over" point making the different gender contracts of the European countries visible:

> For 'reconciling paid work and family life' means more than increasing women's access to paid work...it instead implies a redistribution of work and status between women and men, that is, changing the gender contract (Duncan 2002: 307).

Stratigaki (2004) provides a more critical analysis of the term arguing that as the dominant policy paradigm in the European social policy changes from regulation in the 1980s to coordination and monitoring in the 1990s, The EU texts shift from using "sharing" language to embracing "reconciling" as framework. The objective of challenging the gendered distribution of care work can be expressed as sharing of family responsibilities, or as reconciliation of work and family life. Stratigaki (2004) emphasizes that sharing is associated more with equality of men and women, while reconciliation is derived from labour market analysis and has a more economic orientation.

Stratigaki's content analysis of EU acts shows how the concept of "reconciliation" which was introduced to encourage gender equality in the labour market, gradually shifted in meaning from an objective with feminist potential (sharing family responsibilities between men and women) to a market-oriented objective (encouraging flexible forms of employment):

Reconciliation, reformulated to mean improving women's ability to combine paid work and family work in their own lives, eventually became an integral part of the EU employment policy in the late 1990s, but reconciliation now served the goal of legitimating more flexible work conditions rather than changing gender relations within the family (Stratigaki 2004: 32).

According to Stratigaki, if it is not targeted specifically at men, reconciliation ceases even to be an equality policy, and ends up simply being a policy to help women find easier ways of shouldering the double burden of combining employment with parenting.

Similarly, Lombardo and Meier (2006) argue that EU documents on work–family reconciliation limit themselves to equal opportunities in the labour market, facilitating a focus on a non-feminist perception of reconciliation (ibid.: 158). EU policies seem more concerned with macroeconomic issues and demographics than gender equality.

A report published by EIRO (The European Foundation for the Improvement of Living and Working Conditions) entitled *Reconciliation of Work and Family Life and Collective Bargaining in the EU*[2] documents this shift from a focus on sharing of family responsibilities and support for childcare to more emphasis on labour market flexibility strategies:

> Following much political debate (at various levels), the term 'reconciliation of work and family life' has come to be used in relation to employment policies more so than equality issues (policies to reconcile family and work life at national or company level may not necessarily address gender segregation within the family) (EIRO 2006: 1)

The same report lists a range of topics as elements of work–family reconciliation strategies including, part-time working, flexitime, special leave and career breaks, compressed working week, job sharing, home-working or teleworking. This list makes it clear that most of the policies on the agenda are formulated to enable flexible working and some serve the priorities of the employers better than helping work–family reconciliation of the employees.

In the feminist literature, it is vital to mention fathers' parental leave options and their involvement in childcare when discussing problems of reconciling work and family for both parents. In her concluding chapter in one of the most comprehensive anthologies on work–family reconciliation and EU policies edited by Linda Hantrais (2000), Monica Threlfall underlines the centrality of fathers when discussing reconciliation policies:

---

2   Available online at: http://www.eiro.eirofound.eu.int.

> If such policies are not targeted at fathers, they end up simply being policies to
> help women find easier ways of shouldering the double burden of combining
> employment with parenting, while allowing fathers to continue as before
> (Threlfall 2000: 187).

Reviewing the different country and policy-based models of reconciliation and
outcomes of these policies, Threlfall proposes five hypothetical models drawn up
from a user's perspective:

- **Model 1**: Public provision of wages for mother's work and care:
  Introducing a mothers' wage for women who are homemakers,
- **Model 2**: The privately contracted homemaker-partner: A variant of the
  first model which involves modernizing aspects of the legal framework of
  marriage so that full-time homemakers and breadwinner spouses hold a
  contract resembling that of the employee and employer,
- **Model 3**: The principal earner plus a secondary earner, customarily
  referred to as the one-and-a-half breadwinner model,
- **Model 4:** Two breadwinners: Both parents work full-time using extensive
  childcare services,
- **Model 5:** The double half-carer, half-provider: Both parents share
  employment and care work (Threlfall 2000: 190-195).

The models specified above make clear the feminist ways of approaching work–
family reconciliation are fundamentally different than flexibility approaches since
they put the emphasis on the unpaid care and household work done by mothers and
offer different ways of valuing it and changing its gendered division:

> In the domestic battle to embed equality and reconcile paid work and family
> life, two key areas for action stand out: The role of employers and that of fathers
> (Threlfall 2000: 200).

The late 2000s witnessed another development showing that the potential
dangers stated by feminist researchers started to emerge at the EU level. The
2008 Commission Report on Equality between men and women uses the term
"reconciling professional and private life" instead of the well established term
work and family (EC 2008). This is probably due to the fact that many individuals
who are not parents or who do not live in families also need a balanced professional
and private life. But for this step to include all employers irrespective of their
family status also means that the possibility of targeting the gendered division of
unpaid work within the families is lost on the way.

The same report states that despite efforts of promoting a fairer gendered
division of childcare there is a significant gender gap in this field. The report shows
evidence of this in the sharp fall in the employment rate for women with young

children (-13.6 points on average), while the rate for men is rising. The employment rate for women with dependent children is only 62.4 per cent compared with 91.4 per cent for men, displaying a difference of 29 points (EC 2008: 5).

The report discusses quality services making for reconciliation of work and private life (EC 2008: 8) arguing that the possibility of reconciling professional life and private life depends both on modern work organization (combining flexibility and security, taking account of gender) and on the availability of accessible and affordable quality services.

The report specifies key challenges for policy:

> Gender gaps remain wide, especially differences in working arrangements between women and men (for example the use of part-time employment and fixed-term contracts, or lower-quality jobs with less pay), horizontal and vertical labour market segregation remains and is even increasing in certain countries, and the pay gap is not getting any narrower (EC 2008: 7).

The 2008 European Commission report on equality between women and men ends mentioning that special attention should be focused on:

- creating more and better jobs for women,
- including a gender perspective in all aspects of job quality,
- improving both the supply and quality of services helping to reconcile professional and private life for both men and women,
- tackling stereotypes in education, employment and the media and emphasizing the role of men in promoting equality,
- developing tools to assess the impact of policies from the gender perspective (EC 2008: 9).

A multifaceted focus is needed to promote gender equality in different life spheres. This encompassing view on gender equality takes the name of "mainstreaming" in the EU policy agenda.

Gender Mainstreaming

Gender mainstreaming first appeared after the 3rd UN World Conference on Women in 1985 as a necessary action to ensure full integration of women's values into development work. The European Commission made a contribution to the preparations for the UN Conference in 1995 and included "mainstreaming equality" in the "Platform for Action" (Booth and Bennett 2002: 438).

Sweden had insisted on the inclusion of mainstreaming as an EU-priority for the UN World Conference. With its inclusion in the UN document, mainstreaming emerged as a major strategy to promote equal opportunities for women and men in the global arena.

Mainstreaming was formally acknowledged in the 3rd Action Programme for Equal Opportunities (1991-1995). The systematic consideration of the differences between the conditions and needs of women and men in all Community policies and actions is the basic feature of the principle of mainstreaming. In the EU documents, mainstreaming is defined as follows:

> Gender mainstreaming is the integration of the gender perspective into every stage of policy processes—design, implementation, monitoring and evaluation—with a view to promoting equality between women and men. It means assessing how policies impact on the life and position of both women and men—and taking responsibility to re-address them if necessary. This is the way to make gender equality a concrete reality in the lives of women and men creating space for everyone within the organizations as well as in communities—to contribute to the process of articulating a shared vision of sustainable human development and translating it into reality (EC nd).

Mainstreaming has increased the number of actors concerned with equal opportunities, since all Directorate Generals are now involved in gender equality policy. However, the concept itself has been widely ambiguous in most national contexts. As many experts in this field argue (e.g. Stratigaki 2005, Lombardo and Meier 2006) the concept is widely misunderstood, at times deliberately misused, and there is urgent need for academic involvement in the discussions around mainstreaming. In the following section, I will review selected feminist work on mainstreaming to provide deeper insight into its conceptualization and implementation in different local contexts.

Feminist Evaluations of Gender Mainstreaming

As Linda Hantrais mentioned in an earlier account of this policy development, there are different feminist reactions to mainstreaming:

> [Mainstreaming] could be interpreted as a sign that governments have acknowledged the wisdom of recognizing the contribution made by women to economic and social life. Alternatively, it could be seen as a means of pacifying women's lobbies by giving the impression that gender issues are being taken into account, but without necessarily formulating and implementing binding legislation (Hantrais 2000: 1).

Throughout the 2000s, various feminist assessments of gender mainstreaming have been published. In this section, I will provide brief reviews of selected work in this field in order to highlight different aspects of this specific EU policy.

Those who are critical of this strategy generally argue that it will be used as a backlash instrument to dissolve women specific structures among the EU institutions. The more optimistic feminist voices in the field tend to underline the importance of a "dual strategy" meaning that positive action measures and budget allocations specifically targeted to equal opportunities should complement the mainstreaming approach.

Mainstreaming is not a goal in its own right, but a necessary mechanism for achieving gender equality through the objectives of other agendas. One of the strengths of mainstreaming may lie in its ability to appeal to politicians at either end of the political spectrum (Booth and Bennett 2002, 443).

Using the metaphor of a "three-legged equality stool" Booth and Bennett (2002) argue that a mainstreaming strategy is dependent on three important supports: The equal treatment perspective, the women's perspective and the gender perspective:

> The equal treatment perspective describes actions that guarantee women the same rights and the same opportunities as men in the public sphere...The women's perspective inspires initiatives that recognize women as a disadvantaged group in society, who deserve particular treatment...Lastly, the gender perspective promotes actions that aim to transform the organization of society to a fairer distribution of human responsibilities...If any of the 'supports' of the stool are weak the potential for the achievement of equality is undermined (ibid.: 434).

According to Booth and Bennett (2002) the lack of acknowledgement of the interdependence of the equality perspectives has resulted in misconception and confused practice. The authors are also critical of the liberal orientation which tends to attribute gender inequality to certain economic requirements. They claim that the gender perspective, which provided the context for the development of mainstreaming, implicitly relies on a liberal conception of social arrangements, which attributes inequality to institutional habit and current economic requirements (Booth and Bennett 2002: 441).

In 2005, the Journal *Social Politics: International Studies in Gender, State and Society* issued a special number on gender mainstreaming which brought together major contributions that contribute significantly to a theoretical clarification of the term and investigate different practices of mainstreaming in different countries (e.g. Walby 2005, Verloo 2005 and Daly 2005a).

In her introductory article to this issue, Sylvia Walby (2005) provides a comprehensive review of the "productive tensions in theory and practice:"

> As a practice, gender mainstreaming is a process to promote gender equality. It is also intended to improve the effectivity of mainline policies by making visible the gendered nature of assumptions, processes, and outcomes...As a form of theory, gender mainstreaming is a process of revision of key concepts to grasp more adequately a world that is gendered, rather than the establishment of a separatist gender theory (Walby 2005: 321).

Walby is in general optimistic about gender mainstreaming and sees it as a powerful development in feminist theory and practice. Even though it is an "essentially contested" concept, the debates on it position "inequality and difference at the heart of social and political theory of state and democracy" (Walby 2005: 339).

In her contribution to this special issue on gender mainstreaming, Mary Daly (2005a) assesses the progress and impact of gender mainstreaming in selected eight countries (Belgium, France, Greece, Ireland, Lithuania, Spain, Sweden an the UK) based on findings from an EU-funded study (EQUAPOL).

One general pattern she mentions is that countries are spreading responsibility for gender across units or departments. Daly also mentions that there is a tendency of "technocratization" mainly understood as gender impact assessment of policies and budgets (ibid.: 436).

Based on this analysis, Daly identifies three varieties of a gender mainstreaming approach:

- Integrated approach (Found only in Sweden).
- Limited transversality (or "mainstreaming light"): This indicates little more than involvement of different government departments in the implementation of a program around gender equality. (Belgium and Ireland are examples)
- Fragmented: Indicating that mainstreaming is confined to a small number of policy domains (France and the UK exemplify this approach) (ibid.: 438-439).

In seven out of eight countries studied, gender mainstreaming does not depart from an analysis of gender inequality as a structural problem. Sweden appears as an exception in this study since it has an entire "package" in place in the sense of an acceptance of the analysis of gender equality, as well as the integration of the full spectrum of relevant procedures for gender mainstreaming across levels of administration (ibid.: 436).

The study shows that the single most widespread motivation for mainstreaming is a wish or compulsion to update gender equality policy:

> In a context where gender mainstreaming is seen, and promoted by the EU especially, as the best [practice] approach, the primary incentive for countries to engage with gender mainstreaming is to 'modernize' their gender equality approach and architecture in that direction (Daly 2005a: 440).

Daly underlines the lack of clarity in the concept and thinks that this is causal since it provides fertile ground for political expediency: "Because mainstreaming is so elastic, it is easy to make a claim to be doing mainstreaming" (Daly 2005a: 439).

Daly claims that the concept has a "fuzzy core" (ibid.: 445) and argues that there is an urgent need to develop theory and specify the core of the approach in sociological terms:

> One of the most important questions that has to be (re)visited is how gender mainstreaming as theory conceives of and relates to gender equality as a societal phenomenon. In this regard...the relationships between state...and society... need further elaboration (Daly 2005a: 449).

Another important critical voice in the field of EU's gender equality policies, Maria Stratigaki (2005), analyses "Gender mainstreaming vs. Positive action" as an ongoing conflict in EU gender policy. Based on an analysis of EU policy documents, Stratigaki seeks to explain how positive action was sidelined after the launch of gender mainstreaming as a result of the specific way gender mainstreaming was used by the opponents of gender equality.

> Gender mainstreaming is the equality policy strategy that has been most critically assessed by feminists and women's organizations, who have pointed to the risks if the conditions for its success are not met and to the increasing evidence of significant weaknesses in its implementation (Stratigaki 2005, 167).

Similar to her detailed analysis of the cooptation of the feminist concepts in the case of work–family reconciliation, Stratigaki's analysis displays controversies and negotiations around the development of mainstreaming policy and demonstrates the importance of the agency of key women politicians. Her analysis shows the power of "the high and middle management of a bureaucratic structure, which drafted documents, selected words, manipulated meanings, delegated powers to individuals and shaped women's constituencies' expectations" (2005, 181).

Stratigaki thinks that a key problem with gender mainstreaming (GM) is that it clashes with dominant policy frames of the EU:

Analysis of the barriers to implementing GM shows that the problem was not that it was newly established and needed a 'period of grace' for policy actors to assimilate it. Barriers are primarily erected because GM is infiltrated by feminist concerns suggesting fundamental changes in ways of thinking and understanding society. However, this policy goal interferes and clashes with other dominant policy frames of the EU based on hierarchical gender distribution of power (Stratigaki 2005, 181).

Lombardo and Meier (2006) provide another analysis which shows that there are inconsistencies and ambiguities in EU policies that challenge a feminist potential. Based on findings from a larger EU project MAGEEQ ("Policy Frames and Implementation Problems: The Case of Gender Mainstreaming") analysing the policy frames operating in a broad range of EU official policy documents, Lombardo and Meier (2006) claim that the definition of gender mainstreaming of the Council of Europe is an "empty signifier"—it focuses on the procedural changes gender mainstreaming involves but does not address what we should understand by a gender equality perspective (ibid.: 152).

In a following publication, Lombardo and Meier (2008) analyse the "evolution" of EU discourse on gender equality from equal opportunities to gender mainstreaming and claim that "the broadening of EU gender equality policy discourse did not entail its deepening" and "has not provided the binding measures necessary for a more effective enforcement of the new equality policy areas" (Lombardo and Meier 2008: 119). The authors argue that the rhetoric on gender mainstreaming has not been supported by legally binding measures but has privileged soft law instruments. This leads to serious implementation concerns:

> ...there are no concrete objectives, no allocation of economic and human resources...no timetable for action, no specific measures for implementing gender mainstreaming, monitoring its application, and sanctioning incompliant actors (Lombardo and Meier 2008: 105).

Conclusions: A Cautious Optimism?

As the review of gender policies of the EU and their various assessments shows, feminists are divided with respect to their general perception and evaluation of the European Union and its policies. Those who are critical of the neoliberal "equal opportunities" approach to the issue of gender equality argue that policies which do not focus on the centrality of the gendered division of care work and the need to share family responsibilities end up becoming market-oriented policies that encourage flexible forms of employment. For example, based on her critical and in-depth analyses of the developments related to "work–family reconciliation" and "gender mainstreaming" Maria Stratigaki (2004, 2005) argues that the feminist potential of both concepts were eventually lost.

EU gender policy has been predominantly based on the strategy of equal opportunities: Equal pay, equal treatments in employment and in social security are the main areas covered by EU gender directives (Lombardo 2003). The main limitation of the focus on equal opportunities is that it tackles "the symptoms but not causes of gender inequality" (Lombardo 2003: 161).

Based on her critical analysis of the EU policies on motherhood and employment Roberta Guerrina (2002) warns that EU policies continue to promote a concept of equality that is biased in favour of legal rights:

> This continued focus on formal rights has occurred at the expense of a more comprehensive approach to gender and the construction of gender roles. One further danger with this approach is that it can pigeonhole the issues of leave and care as 'women's issues', ultimately reaffirming traditional gender divisions of labour and the male breadwinner model of welfare (Guerrina 2002: 64).

Those who are more optimistic about the potential of EU gender policy underline a basic evolution that took place in EU gender policies from a focus on women's issues to an acknowledgment of gender relations and the need to transform the traditional gender contract.

For example, Angelika Von Wahl (2005) argues that EU policy moved from a standard of gender sameness to the inclusion of women's difference and a European equal employment regime has taken a permanent hold with the EU (ibid.: 90).

In her more optimistic approach, Sylvia Walby (2004) argues that a distinct, gender regime is developing in the EU in which women's access to employment is facilitated by the removal of discrimination, regulation of working time to be compatible with caring and policies to promote social inclusion. Walby underscores the important development that although employment has been the focus of the initiatives for gender equality, gender policies have "migrated" into many other areas and led to policy "innovations" concerning issues of fertility, sexuality and violence against women (Walby 2004: 20).

My own position on the gender policies of the EU can be labelled a cautious optimism. The analysis above shows that these policies are not coherent and are marked with contrasting tendencies. Key social actors in EU institutions have fought to put forward gender equality policies in a context dominated by economic concerns and an "identity crisis" for the EU itself. These policies do make a change especially in the countries which historically have a hostile attitude towards feminism and rely on traditional familialistic policies. Bringing gender equality discussions into the public agenda is an important step even though there are serious implementation problems. The analysis in the next chapter will discuss these issues in light of empirical findings form an EU funded international study which focused on transition to parenthood in different workplace contexts.

Chapter 5
Work–Family Reconciliation
in Practice

As the review of gender policies of the European Union in the former chapter made apparent, the issue of reconciling family and work responsibilities is now conceptualized as a key component of the gender equality agenda. The EU endorses a basic "package" focussing on parental leave, institutional childcare and flexibility. However, the existing policies as well as attitudes concerning work–family issues show a significant variation throughout Europe. The dominant gender regime in a given country, relative strength of the women's movement, demographic patterns and economic conditions all interact and influence how EU policies are conceived and implemented locally.

In order to understand the operation of specific policies in practice one needs access to first hand accounts of individuals gathered in a context sensitive manner. In this chapter the focus will be a discussion of work–family reconciliation in light of qualitative data compiled for an EU-funded international research project.

As work–family reconciliation became a popular theme on the EU policy agenda, the European Commission funded several cross-national research projects that aim to assess policy implications and practices in different local contexts. One such project funded by the Fifth Framework Programme of the European Commission was entitled: "Gender, Parenthood and the Changing European Workplace: Young Adults Negotitating the Work–Family Boundary (Transitions)."

The Transitions project was coordinated by Suzan Lewis at Manchester Metropolitan University and Janet Smithson was the project manager.[1] It started in January 2003 and was completed in December 2005. I was involved in this project throughout the whole period as a postdoctoral research fellow in the Norwegian research team led by Ann Nilsen. In this chapter, I will first present some of the general findings of this project from its different research phases. I will then focus on a three-country comparison based on case studies carried out in a number of

---

1   See project website at http://www.workliferesearch.org/transitions for a complete list of project partners. I acknowledge the key contribution of the whole research team for the data and analysis presented in this chapter. Special thanks to the project coordinator Suzan Lewis, project manager Janet Smithson and to the coordinator of the Norwegian team Ann Nilsen.

social services offices in Norway, the UK and Portugal and discuss issues related to work–family reconciliation in light of qualitative data.

Transitions Project: A Context Sensitive Cross-national Study

Transitions was a qualitative research project that examined how young European men and women (aged 25-40) working in public and private sector workplaces manage work–family reconciliation in the contexts of different welfare state regimes, family and workplace support. Eight European countries participated in the project: United Kingdom, Norway, France, Portugal, Sweden, The Netherlands, Bulgaria and Slovenia. The national research teams consisted of a research partner and a senior researcher (or several research fellows). Over twenty researchers from the eight countries made up a lively interdisciplinary team. The team adopted a multi-method strategy to answer its key research questions focussing on gendered aspects of work–family issues.

A central aim of this project has been to study how factors at different levels— national, organizational and personal—influence the situations of mothers and fathers employed at specific workplaces. Another aim was to study how type of work sector (public or private) affects employees' experiences of work–family reconciliation.

The Transitions project consisted of three research phases. The first phase involved contextual mapping of the national policy and demographic context and an extensive literature review. In the second phase, case studies were carried out in one public sector (social services) and one private sector (mostly finance) organization. A key objective of the organizational case studies was to examine the characteristics of workplace change to analyse how these are reflected in workplace policies influencing work–family reconciliation practices of young parents (Guerreira et al. 2004). Methods used included focus groups with parents, interviews with managers and document analysis. The third phase consisted of in-depth, biographical interviews with parents and drew its sample mainly from the focus groups. A primary objective of the interview study was to gain an understanding of motherhood and fatherhood from a gendered perspective. This involved examining the transition to parenthood by adopting a life course perspective combined with a biographical approach (Nilsen and Brannen 2005).

A multi-method strategy was adopted in this cross-national study. Three dimensions have been important for the methodological design: Case study logic, life course perspective and a biographical approach. This methodological approach enabled us to link the micro-level of the individual working parent's life to the wider structural and historical context (Nilsen and Brannen 2005).

The first phase of the study resulted in two major research reports at the end of the first year: The *Literature Review* edited by the Dutch team (den Dulk et al 2003) and the *Context Mapping* report, compiled and edited by the French team (Fagnani et al. 2003).[2] The main objective of the literature review was an evaluation of recent European literature (since 1998) on organizational, gender and well-being issues in relation to the transition to parenthood and the negotiations of work–family boundaries. The *Literature Review* is published online by the European Community Research and Development Information Service (CORDIS) as "State of the Art Report" of the Transitions project.[3]

The aim of the context mapping was to give a broad outline of the principal economic, social and demographic characteristics of the eight countries. The Context Mapping Report starts by comparing economic indicators of wealth and social inequality and shows that Norway, followed by the Netherlands and Sweden, is the wealthiest country while Bulgaria is the poorest with a GNP per citizen nearly six times smaller than that of Norway (Fagnani et al. 2003: 13). The Scandinavian countries demonstrate lower indicators of social inequality, while the United Kingdom and Portugal show the highest levels of social inequality by the same measures.

The second part of the report is devoted to a comprehensive description of childcare and parental leave policies in each country. The analysis shows that Sweden, Norway, France and Slovenia display especially higher support levels while the United Kingdom and the Netherlands are distinguished by the less supportive political and social attitudes they demonstrate in policies that affect new parents and small children. The report also highlights an increasing similarity in length of parental leave due to recent developments in European Union legislation (Fagnani et al. 2003: 14).

The report also provides a comparative study of birth rates and shows that irrespective of the statistical indicator used, whether the "total fertility rate" or "completed fertility rate," France and Norway are the countries with the highest birth rates, while Bulgaria and Slovenia are at the other end of the scale. Analysing women's participation patterns in the labour market, the report shows that the rates of employment of women between the ages of 25 and 49 has increased in all the countries in line with investments in education, but underlines a key variation:

> Apart from in Portugal and Slovenia, young women with children often work
> on a part-time basis. In Sweden and in France, women typically work 'long part
> time hours' compared to the 'short part time hours' of women in the Netherlands

---

2   The full context mapping report is available online at: http://www.workliferesearch. org/transitions/mapping.html.

3   Available online at: http://cordis.europa.eu/citizens/publications.htm#stateoftheart.

or the United Kingdom. In terms of the number of hours spent at work, the differences between the sexes are apparent whichever country we considered but it is in the Netherlands and the United Kingdom that these differences are most marked (Fagnani et al 2003: 15).

The report also focuses on dominant values and norms with respect to obligations of parents and the needs of children. Concerning the theoretical preferences for balancing work and home life for the age group 25-39, a majority of those living in France, the United Kingdom, Slovenia and Portugal said they would prefer "to have a full time job and more than one child." The same age group living in Sweden and the Netherlands replied "a part time job and more than one child" (Fagnani et al. 2003: 16). This exemplifies the different gendered ideologies and expectations, as well as different structural possibilities for work–family arrangements, prevailing in these countries.

The Context Mapping Report ends with a summary of key similarities among the eight European countries of the Transitions project:

- Increase in female education attainment levels;
- Increase in mothers' labour force participation rates;
- Enduring gender asymmetry in family involvement;
- Development of family-friendly measures (increase in the number of employer-based work/family policies and development of public child care provision);
- Polarization: Strong divide between highly-educated women and low-skilled women;
- Below replacement fertility rates, except for France and Norway. (Fagnani et al 2003: 177).

The report also attempts to integrate mother's employment patterns and major ways of combining paid and unpaid work identifying three major models: Norway and Sweden exemplify the "egalitarian model" due to the extensive availability of public schemes supporting working parents. The UK and the Netherlands are categorized as "modified male breadwinner" models due to prevalence of short part-time jobs for mothers. France, Portugal, Slovenia and Bulgaria are all different examples for different forms of the "dual-earner model" in which both parents work long hours using diverse combinations for childcare (Fagnani et al. 2003: 178).

The extensive literature review and the context mapping exercise provided us with the necessary background knowledge for a context-sensitive analysis of the qualitative data that we would collect in the second and third phases.

Organizational Case Studies: Analysing Workplace Policies and Practices

In the organizational case study phase, we chose workplaces in private and public sectors. In Portugal, the UK, Bulgaria and Norway two case studies were carried out in one public sector and one private sector organization. In the Netherlands and Slovenia only one private sector organization was studied, while the case study in Sweden took place only in the public sector.

A main purpose of the organizational case studies was to gain an in-depth understanding of the various supports and constraints that are in action for the working parents. The policies and practices that prevail were approached both from the perspectives of the managers and employees. The whole research team discussed the interview guides to be used for manager interviews and the focus groups and the questions were standardized by careful translations into local languages to enhance cross-national comparisons.

The first contact into the organizations was achieved through the project partners sending an information letter signed by the project coordinator. The Human Resources manager or another top manager was contacted and informed about this international research project. This manager usually guided us to a middle manager or unit managers to arrange the details of the Focus Group and other manager interviews.

A total of 68 focus groups, consisting of 281 parents, were conducted for the Transitions project (Guerreiro et al. 2004: 20). Only 27 per cent of the participants were fathers and the rest were mothers. There were more fathers in the private sector companies and fewer in the social services, reflecting the fact that social services are heavily female dominated in all participating countries (Guerreiro et al. 2004).

Focus groups were useful in the organizational case study phase because our main intention was to get an impression of how employees at the same workplace talked about the issues that concerned our study in a collective setting. In order to achieve a satisfactory level for cross-national comparisons, teams adapted the focus group schedules, broadly sticking to the order of topics and key questions. The national research teams compiled and analysed data following a standardized framework.[4] The framework specified the following sections for detailed analysis:

1. Organizational Context
   Workforce profile, absenteeism, sickness rates, employment contracts, trade unions, etc.

---

4   The framework was discussed in the project meetings and finalised by the UK/ London research team led by Julia Brannen.

2. Workplace Policies

Equal opportunities policies, working hours policies, leave policies for parents, etc.

3. Workplace Practices, Cultures, and Implementation of Workplace Policies

Examples of some key questions we sought to answer in this section: Are workplace policies implemented in respect of parents? How are they implemented? How family friendly are the policies?

Examples of good and bad management practice—in relation to employees seeking to meet routine family responsibilities and family crises. How important are managers in relation to workplace policies?

4. Organizational Change

Changes in numbers of personnel, working hours, wage rates, staff contracts, nature and organization of work, etc.

How are employees' work orientations being reshaped by organizational change? Communication and implementation of changes.

Managers and employees as agents and recipients of change.

5. Organizational well-being

Employer as a caring organization, team building, identification with the organization, etc.

6. Parents and Individual well-being

Feelings of work intensification, job insecurity, trust, etc.

7. Work–Family strategies and boundary negotiation

Ways of managing work and child care responsibilities, blurring of work-home boundaries, etc.

8. Methodological issues

Reflections on negotiating access, interview encounter and interactions.

National teams analysed and wrote their national case study reports following the general framework summarized above. The Norwegian team prepared two separate reports, one for the private sector company (with the pseudonym NMC) and one for social services (Nilsen, Sümer and Granlund 2004). The Portuguese research team, led by Maria das Dores Guerreiro, compiled the national reports to prepare the consolidated case studies report which was published in 2004.[5] The consolidated report attempts to present the findings that are common in most of the countries and to consider some of the key differences.

A general review of the national case studies shows that feelings of work intensification were widespread throughout all the organizations studied (Guerreiro et al. 2004: 12). One of the major consequences of work intensification is the growing practice of putting in long hours, intruding on time and energy for families.

---

5   The executive summary of this report is available at the project homepage.

There are different national policies with respect to work–family reconciliation that are in action in the eight countries: Length of paid parental leave; possibilities of part-time work and public support for childcare vary significantly (although there is a convergence induced by changing EU legislation).

The involvement of the welfare state in the regulation of the labour market shows variation:

> In Nordic countries (Norway and Sweden) the welfare state is traditionally very strong, having a greater responsibility and an important role in organizations and organization of working life, and provides concrete measures which are tightly implemented...In contrast, in the UK, the Netherlands and Portugal, public legislation leaves a higher degree of freedom to organizations. In Bulgaria and Slovenia, a traditional vision of state primacy coexists with emerging liberal and individualized trends. Recent public measures on work-life reconciliation frequently utilize the rhetoric of flexibility—plans, orientations, good practices and so on—in order to encourage organizations to change while leaving them the ultimate power to decide (Guerreiro et al. 2004: 23).

A common finding that applies to all countries is that there is an implementation gap (in varying degrees) between formal policies and current practices. Managers play a decisive role in the implementation of the law. The case studies also showed that colleagues have an important role in parents' negotiations related to work–family reconciliation, especially in the context of intense workloads where parents working flexibly or taking leaves can intensify colleagues' overload.

A major finding of all the case studies is the considerable gap between workplace formal policies and actual practices. Despite national social policies and organizational policies, daily workplace practices appear to be most influenced by informal strategies and interactions, shaped by local workplace cultures:

> It is notable that in Norway and Sweden, where social policies are better, there is less pressure on individual employees and their line managers to work out individualized solutions to family and paid work demands. In Portugal, where there is no security net provided by a welfare state, these negotiations take on a more vital role. However, workplace policies and their implementation by managers are demonstrated in the case studies to be important even in the Scandinavian contexts, in encouraging the actual take-up of policies, for example the father's part of parental leaves (Guerreiro et al. 2004: 36).

Employees' entitlements tend to be interpreted in a different manner among different occupational groups, especially in Portugal, the United Kingdom and the Netherlands. Employees' statutory entitlements tend to vary according to the nature of the work, professional status, type of contracts and access to information

(Guerreiro et al. 2004: 25). Employees with temporary contracts feel especially restricted and often refrain from making use of their statutory entitlements.

The use of leaves provided by law is a complex process involving "mixed arrangements" that is a combination of formal and informal negotiations. Statutory maternity leaves are the most accepted arrangement:

> According to the case studies, maternity leave appears to be almost fully used in social services and in most private companies in all the countries. In Sweden, Norway, Slovenia and Bulgaria, this leave is taken for granted. However, there is evidence that managers in private companies in other countries use 'silent strategies' to undermine this entitlement in order to meet organizational goals and tasks, especially in periods of work overload (Guerreiro et al. 2004: 60).

A common pattern around Europe appears to be that work–family reconciliation policies are implicitly targeting women despite gender-neutral discourse. In Dutch, Norwegian, Swedish and British organizations, it is common that women workers (especially those in the public sector) reduce their work schedules to part-time work when they have small children (Guerreiro et al. 2004: 28).

The case studies documented significant differences between policies, cultures and practices of private and public sectors across the seven countries, although both sectors are experiencing changes that are blurring the traditional contrasts between them. There is a stronger commitment to national legislation in the public organizations. For example, working hours, annual and parental leaves are better implemented. In private organizations, formal legislation is implemented in a more flexible way and negotiated individually with employees. The general intention in the private sector is the attempt to unite employees' entitlements with organizational needs:

> In the private organizations, workplace conditions are often considerably better than in the public sector ones—higher salaries, training opportunities and other fringe benefits—but work overload is common and pressure to not use entitlements when not convenient for the companies is higher. In the social services, managers and employees face many dilemmas and stresses caused by lack of resources, but they tend to feel they are privileged in terms of schedules and leaves and, therefore, they feel relatively well supported in the reconciliation of employment and family life (especially women) (Guerreiro et al. 2004: 42).

The Transitions case studies consolidated report ends with a discussion of the problems and issues related to conceptualization of "organizational well-being." The report points at the diverging approaches to the concept of well-being from the perspective of managers and employees and underscores that organizational well-being cannot be compared in an objective or straightforward way across organizations and cross nationally because of the complex values and processes involved in defining the situations (Guerreiro et al. 2004: 47).[6]

Upon completing organizational case studies, the Transitions team moved on to the third and final phase of the project, namely the biographical interview study.

Interview Study: An In-depth Analysis of Working Parents' Lives

The focus group interviews had ended with a question to the participants about their wish to be personally interviewed in a later phase of the Transitions study. A good number of the focus group participants agreed to a personal interview and were contacted about ten months after the organizational case study.

A main objective of the interview study was to gain an understanding of motherhood and fatherhood from a gendered perspective. This involved examining the transition to parenthood of both men and women. The analysis of the interviews also focused on the experiences of being a working parent in the present and the major sources of support and constraints for mothers and fathers. The consolidated interview report was compiled by Ann Nilsen and Julia Brannen (2005) drawing on the national reports from seven countries.[7]

The consolidated interview report states that the general approach adopted in the analysis represents a way of linking the micro level of the individual working parent's life to the wider structural and historical context: "in particular the macro level of the national context but also the meso level of organizations, kinship networks and local services" (Nilsen and Brannen 2005: 17).

In the interview study report, biographical interviews were analysed comparatively through selected cases:

Cases were selected *purposively*...The analysis and presentation of a case based on biographical methods shows how, in the detail of the case, a trajectory is created, shaped and made sense of by the person. Cases used comparatively can demonstrate typicality. In *replicating* cases—selecting similar cases to see if the same phenomena are found under similar conditions—it is possible to see if a pattern holds across more than one case...The logic of case study does not make

---

6 Examining the concept of positive well-being has been an important component of the Transitions project but I will not dwell on this part of the study in this chapter. The executive summary of the well-being report is available at the project website.

7 Executive summary of the interview study report is available online at the project website.

claims appealing to statistical representativeness but does so through theoretical
argument (Nilsen and Brannen 2005: 29, emphases original).

Throughout the report, different experiences of transition to parenthood, current
experiences of being a working parent and different types of supports and constraints
for parents are highlighted through in-depth analyses of biographical interviews.
Thick comparisons of selected cases demonstrate how different regimes of working
hours and different forms of formal and informal childcare create complex webs
of support for parents of young children across the seven countries (Nilsen and
Brannen 2005: 75). These detailed analyses cannot be adequately summarized in
this context. I will only mention some of the findings pertaining to work–family
reconciliation policies.

In the interview analyses, the most significant support for working parents
appeared as quality childcare and possibilities of reducing working hours. The
report underlines that part-time work, where it exists, is largely an option for
mothers and this has direct consequences for their further involvement in the labour
market. In conclusion, the report emphasizes the key finding that the transition to
parenthood appears to be a critical "tipping point" on the road to gender equality
and "there is a dilemma that policies that meet parents' currently articulated needs
—for example part-time work for mothers—also reproduce gender inequalities"
(Nilsen and Brannen 2005: 78).

Parallel with the work on biographical interviews, the national research
teams cooperated to prepare a consolidated National Debates Report which
provides an overview of national debates on work and family in the participating
countries and a Good Practice Report that explores employer "good practices"
from the perspective of new parents.[8] The good practices report underlines the
context-specificity of what counts as a good practice and how the workplace
practices are dependent upon the specific organizational cultures. Through
analysis of qualitative data, the report shows that it is possible to pinpoint some
basic principles of good practices, emphasizing implementation of statutory
entitlements, management consistency, colleague support and realistic workloads
(Purcell et al. 2005).

The final report of the Transitions project, which was compiled by the project
coordinator Susan Lewis and the project manager Janet Smithson, summarizes
the key findings of interim reports and provides a synthesis of the main findings
of the project. The final report underscores that experiences of the transition to
parenthood depend on many, interrelated layers of context (Lewis and Smithson
2006). Work–family strategies are developed not only in the context of macro

---

8 Both reports available online at: http://www.workliferesearch.org/transitions/
whatsnew.html.

social policies but also in the context of the rapid transformations in workplaces. The different political contexts and, particularly welfare state policies are shaping different organizational contexts. The most significant policies influencing work–family reconciliation are lengths and payments of parental leaves, childcare options and opportunities to work part time or flexibly. Still the effects of different policies may be undermined by current workplace practices associated with work intensification and concerns for future job opportunities (Lewis and Smithson 2006: 81).

The Transitions study showed that national policies and provisions interact with formal and informal workplace policies, practices and cultures and economic conditions to support and constrain gender expectations and transformations, in complex ways (Lewis and Smithson 2006). For example, national policy has long been based on equal opportunities ideology in Sweden and Norway and also under the former communist regimes in Bulgaria and Slovenia, but the outcomes are very different. In the former Eastern bloc countries women have been disproportionately affected by the transition from a socialist to a market-based economy and they are more vulnerable to unemployment under the new regimes. Besides, the focus is on equality of opportunities for men and women in terms of labour force participation and not gender equity in the home.

The Transitions project findings make clear that national public policies need to be backed up by workplace practice:

> Persisting gendered organizational values and assumptions, such as…that ideal workers do not work part-time…contribute to an implementation gap between policy (national and workplace) and practice in all the case study organizations, albeit to varying extents (Lewis and Smithson 2006: 21).

The final report also points at the seeds of positive change in this field documented by the Transitions project:

> There is evidence of some positive changes but these are often accompanied by transitional tensions as commensurate changes in other layers of context take place more slowly. Examples include the growing involvement of fathers in parenting in Norway and Sweden as a consequence of social policies to support fatehring. This raises expectations of shared parenting, which can create tensions when some employers continue to expect men not to take family leaves…Transitions can create tensions at multiple levels; within individuals as they adapt to changing gender practices and expectations at a personal level; within households as parents adapt relationships at an interpersonal level; and within workplaces…where the pace of change is too rapid or is uneven (Lewis and Smithson 2006: 92).

The final report of the Transitions project ends with a discussion of the implications of these findings for policy by drawing attention to the fundamental tensions between contemporary working patterns and the needs of parents to be able to care for their children. The report underlines the importance of a multi-layered and joined up approach to policy-making and the need for a focus on long-term outcomes:

> Socially sustainable families, workplaces and societies in Europe require long-term thinking as well as interrelated changes at many levels. For example, policies that meet parents' currently articulated needs—such as part-time work—are clearly important for parents' strategies for negotiating work and family boundaries, especially in the context of intensified workloads, but given that it is overwhelmingly mothers who adopt this strategy, it will inevitably reproduce gender inequalities in the longer term in the absence of changes in workplace values and practices (Lewis and Smithson 2006: 95).

The project was completed at the end of 2005 but the national teams continued to cooperate for further comparative analyses which resulted in various publications and papers presented in international conferences.[9] A group within the Transitions team continues to cooperate on another EU-funded project with the title *Quality of Life in a Changing Europe*. Currently, the Transitions team is about to publish the first project book based on comparative analyses of organizational case-studies (Lewis et al. 2009).

In light of these key findings of the Transitions project, I will now move on to a comparative analysis of the work–family reconciliation practices of the parents working at social services in Norway, the UK and Portugal drawing on organizational case studies. The analysis will build on the contextual information and findings of a former three-country comparison of selected cases working at private sector organizations (Sümer et al. 2008). This time the focus will be on the policies and practices at social services offering different supports and constraints for Norwegian, British and Portuguese working parents.

Key Supports and Constraints for the Working Parents at Social Services in Norway, the UK and Portugal[10]

A three country comparison of Norway, the UK and Portugal provides interesting results due to the key contextual differences reflected in the case studies of the Transitions project. This became clear through a former comparative analysis of

---

9   The final Dissemination Report is available online at the project website.

10   The analysis presented here is based on data from the national case study reports (Nilsen et al. 2004, Guerreiro et al 2004 and Brannen et al 2004). Many thanks to the

case study findings in the private sector organizations. This comparison is discussed in detail in an article entitled "Becoming Working Mothers: Reconciling Work and Family at Three Particular Workplaces in Norway, the UK and Portugal" (Sümer et al. 2008). Investigating differences in national and organizational welfare policies and in cultural norms influencing work–family reconciliation for selected cases, the analysis had showed that there were important differences between these three organizations with respect to parents' awareness and use of their statutory rights. The Norwegian employees displayed a very high sense of entitlement and were well informed about their rights as parents of small children. Employees of the British private company had little knowledge of their parental rights and felt guilty of making use of their entitlements. The Portuguese employees were often forced to give up their statutory rights due to high work pressure (Sümer et al. 2008).

How do the employees in social services fare with respect to work–family reconciliation? The case studies that took place at selected units of social services in Norway, the UK and Portugal provide data on the general working environments of these organizations and on specific experiences of reconciling work and family.

The first step in this three-country comparison will be a more detailed analysis of the Norwegian case study in order to highlight the focus of the Transitions project and to discuss how policies are experienced in practice in light of this qualitative data. The second step will be a brief analysis of the wishes that working parents in the three countries express with respect to what can support them in combining work and family.

Norwegian Social Services: Flexible Work and Political Wishes

The Transitions case-study in the social services took place in four units of a local Norwegian Municipality. This is a female dominated field, as in most other European countries. Social workers on the whole have relatively low salaries in the Norwegian context. The turnover and sick leave rates are very high. The average sick leave rate in the Social Services studied was 11 per cent in 2002, which is higher than the Norwegian average of around 7 per cent the same year (Nilsen, Sümer and Granlund 2004: 7). The most important organizational change in Social Services has been merging of units and outsourcing of certain services. A key source of insecurity for employees in this part of the labour market is this ongoing process of "modernization" resulting in major reorganizations and merging of services.

The Municipality in which we had our case-study had a difficult financial situation in recent years, resulting in cuts in the budget. Many social workers

national teams, particularly to project partners Ann Nilsen, Julia Brannen and Maria das Dores Guereiro, for letting me draw on data from national case studies.

interviewed stated that they face the constraints of time and money and often cannot follow up their clients the way they would prefer to (Nilsen et al. 2004).

The Norwegian case study in social services conducted by the Norwegian team (Ann Nilsen, Sevil Sümer and Lise Granlund) consisted of face-to-face interviews with a group of managers, focus group interviews in four different units and an analysis of official documents and reports. We interviewed four unit managers and conducted four Focus Group interviews with a total of eighteen parents.[11] The quotes used in this section are selected from these interviews.

In general, our case study showed that social services were considered "family friendly" by managers and employees alike. Flexibility and understanding offered at the work-place were major factors influencing the lives of parents. It was relatively easy to make use of the entitlements formulated by the welfare state, which comprised among others, reduction in working hours and sick-child leave.

Our interviewees experienced social services as supportive, especially when compared with the private sector jobs. The following quote from a social worker with three children exemplifies this experience:

> I know that the private sector pays more but you must also sacrifice yourself. Municipality has a good attitude concerning family life...and it is not always like that in the private sector. You have your rights but you must fight for them.

A key policy making the lives of parents employed in social services easier is the possibility of arranging their working hours, the policy which is labelled "flexitime."

Reflections on Flexible and Reduced Working Hours

In the Norwegian social services, flexitime means that employees are entitled to flexible working hours within certain regulations. All workers must be present in the office between 9 am and 2 pm but they can arrange their working hours (7.5 hours per day) within the limits of 6 am in the morning and 6 pm in the evening. They are also allowed to work shorter one day as long as they compensate for the missing hours in another day of the week. This policy of flexible working hours was considered a great benefit by the employees as revealed by the following quote from a 34-year-old father with three children:

---

11   Two of the groups consisted of four participants, and two had five participants. Only two fathers participated in the focus groups, compared to sixteen mothers, reflecting the female dominated character of this workplace.

The municipality has a considerate attitude towards parents with young children, and the flexible working hours are absolutely wonderful. I just tell people that today my wife is working nights, and then nobody asks any questions when you leave early as long as you're within the right number of hours per week with the allowed minus time, you can always work more later on so that there is a balance over the month.

Flexitime was often mentioned as the major supportive policy in reconciling work and family obligations. For example, some parents conceived flexitime as a good opportunity to arrange a division of labour between the mother and the father in arranging daily childcare:

The most important is flexible working hours. We have that here, and it's very good. I take my child to the nursery at around eight, and my husband picks her up at three so the child is there maximum seven hours, which is long enough (29 years old mother with 1 child).

A general tendency among Norwegian social workers who participated in the focus groups was to display high expectations with respect to gender equality. An egalitarian division of childcare responsibilities was an often mentioned theme. However, many also pointed at disappointments and remaining gendered patterns with respect to gendered division of care work.

Another gendered pattern often discussed at the focus groups was the practice of part-time working. The possibility of working reduced hours was an often used and discussed policy. Many mothers had experience with part-time work and there were different views on this practice. While some considered this as a good way of finding more time for the family, others argued that part-time work can actually lead to more stress and have negative impact on career prospects:

You feel that…they don't like it that we work reduced hours, the system. People are fine but the system forces you to return to a full time job. Benefits are taken away from you and you don't get the equivalent amount of work. It is difficult to work a reduced number of hours. I always get comments like: 'oh, you are in today, are you working?' All those sarcastic comments when you don't work full time (40 years old mother with 3 children).

In one focus group the negative consequences of reduced working hours were discussed in detail and the participants came up with a number of suggestions for policy changes. A higher awareness of gender inequalities in this respect was apparent in the discussion:

My dream situation is that when you are in a phase with small children, you could work reduced hours and keep the same entitlements as you did when you worked full time. Not a full salary, but the same pension rights. I think most people could handle a small reduction in their salary, but that you lag behind all the time because you're a woman, I think that is a significant problem in society because it is women who work reduced hours. I think it should be treated as full time, because you work full time really, even if you work fewer hours paid (33 years old mother of 2 children).

Men are also working full time, but the women take the part without salary. A solution could be that men pay their wife a part of their salary, when you are married or living together and have kids, so that the pension later would be divided in two (39 years old mother of 2 children).

Discussions related to a more egalitarian sharing of the parental leave were also common themes in the focus groups. As we have seen in Chapter 3, taking at least four weeks paid leave from work to care for their children is now a majority practice among Norwegian fathers. Social services experienced as a flexible workplace that allows fathers to take longer leaves, as was experienced by one of the participants of our case study. Scarcity of public childcare facilities for the youngest children and the problem of long waiting lists to get a place at day-care institutions was a common problem discussed in the focus groups.

Our case study showed that the employees in social services had a tendency of discussing possible political solutions for their work–family reconciliation problems. For example, many argued that a universal 6 hour work day would be a good solution for the so-called "time-squeeze" problem:

There are good arrangements, but at the same time I think that…after I personally reduced my working hours to 80 per cent, that having a 6 hours work day is enough. Because you will both keep yourself above the water and have an OK life, in relation to the kids. So one could work 6 hours a day and earn a full salary…it is expensive to have children in day-care…for example, as long as children were below the age of 15, that you would have the opportunity to work 6 hours, that would be enough. I think that people become more effective within a given domain, instead of contributing 8 or 9 hours.

Time-squeeze is a main dilemma in the lives of our interviewees. Many wish to be active in the labour market and work full-time and this contradicts their ideal of being active parents as well. Those who reduce their working hours either think of this as a temporary solution for their current life-phase, putting off their ambitions at work for a while; or see this as a way of putting the family first, by cutting off their career plans for good.

When asked about their wishes for changes that would make it easier for them to be a working parent, many still mentioned reduced working hours:

If you could wish for something that in future would make it easier for you to combine paid work with being a parent, what would you think of then?

The working hours, definitely. Reduced working hours and flexibility. To be able to come in around nine in the morning and leave around three. Incredible how much time it really would add to the day. That would have been super!

Parents employed in social services display a less individualized outlook on life and often refer to structural constraints or political priorities influencing their lives, compared to the parents employed in the private sector organization. Norwegian social workers who participated in the Transitions project tend to consider their work–family reconciliation problems as a "public issue" which needs to be resolved by political action.

This factor becomes even clearer when compared to the wishes of the British and the Portuguese parents working at social services. Following a brief review of the general findings of the UK and Portuguese case studies in social services with respect to support and constraints on work–family reconciliation, the next section will provide a concise comparison of the parents' wishes on policy or attitude changes that would make their work–family reconciliation easier.

Individualized vs. Political Wishes

The UK Social Services case study which was conducted by the London team (Julia Brannen, Rob Pattman and Michaela Brockmann) was based on eleven manager interviews and eleven focus group interviews including 28 parents (21 mothers and 7 fathers). The UK case study report states that the general terms and conditions of public sector employment are considered more favourable compared with the private sector due to final pension schemes; good holiday entitlement; flexi-time and maternity leave beyond the statutory minimum and relatively well established equal opportunities policies (Brannen et al. 2004: 6).

The UK case study report asserts that all of the Focus Group participants commented on the increased pressure and work intensification. They related this to changes to the job role and increased bureaucracy, increased use of targets, higher case loads, lack of resources, and high staff turnover (Brannen et al. 2004: 8).

Employees' entitlement to a number of workplace policies was affected by length of service, that is those with the longest service had better conditions, for example with respect to maternity leave and annual leave. There were only a few policies which working parents could draw upon for work–family reconciliation: Part-time work, flexitime and five days per annum special leave or dependence leave. In practice, these policies were largely at managers' discretion. Access to them by employees was heavily constrained by the knowledge and willingness of managers to apply these policies and the type of work and service employees worked in:

> If you have a good manager, he can give you compassionate leave. If you have a terrible manager, sorry, you're out of luck (Brannen et al. 2004: 45).

Taking annual leave was a typical solution when people needed a day off for family related concerns. Few people knew about or used dependent's leave which was theoretically a right but was in fact only given at managers' discretion. The case study report also states differences among employees with respect to job status and work–family reconciliation. While those with little autonomy and who worked in front line services had to resort to taking annual leave or sick leave when care responsibilities called them away from work, those more highly qualified workers, for example some social workers, had more autonomy in organizing their work and thus manage the boundaries between home and work better (Brannen et al. 2004: 78).

The wishes most often mentioned by the focus group participants that were related to ways of making social services more family friendly for parents with young children included longer paid parental leave; financial or other incentives to attract people into social services and to keep them in their employment; an end to manager inflexibility; the importance of making clear to employees which workplace policies there are and not having to take annual leave or sick leave to meet family commitments (Brannen et al. 2004: 51).

The British case study in social services clearly shows the more individualized atmosphere concerning work–family reconciliation which opens a larger room for manager discretion. In this context, a general wish stated by the employees to ease work–family reconciliation was "more flexibility" as put by a single mother who had an especially long travel distance to work:

> …a bit more flexibility in the sense that…when you start somewhere, it's not easy because…you do nine to five and it's nine to five. You do have to struggle a little bit before there's flexibility sort of comes in. And I think if…you're a working mother, you travel a long way, I think it shouldn't be an issue…But it's not something that's offered to you automatically, 'How can we help you or what can we do to make life easier?' Because if they really want to retain staff I think that's the area, they have to say, 'How can we make things easier for you?,' 'What facilities can we put into place,' as long as you do your hours, you know (Brannen et al. 2004: 50).

The British case study documents the lack of specific family-friendly policies that working parents can draw on and the more individualized solutions that mothers and fathers wish for. This reflects the general tradition of defining family related issues as private problems in the historically liberal welfare model prevailing in the UK (Daly and Rake 2003; Sümer et al. 2008).

The Portuguese Social Services case study which was conducted by the Portuguese team (Maria das Dores Guerreiro, Pedro Abrantes and Inês Pereira) was based on interviews with 6 managers and 7 focus groups in which 18 mothers and 5 fathers participated. The case study report states that in general the Portuguese social services follow the leave policies and entitlements for parents as specified by the law and both the employees and managers feel that implementation of legal entitlements is a great privilege (Guerreiro et al. 2004).

Many workers told that they were satisfied with the management in relation to work–family balance just because they follow legislation, which is quite unusual in some areas of the private sector. Similar to their Norwegian and British counterparts, employees in social services compared their situation to those working in private sector organizations and thought that it was easier for them to reconcile work and family. Especially high-skilled workers, with some experience in the private sector emphasized this aspect:

> Here they try to follow legislation. I remember…I can give you a comparison: When I had my first child, the first year of his life—I was working in a private company—and he was 11 or 12 hours in crèche. This is too much for a baby in his first year! And I see, since the moment I came here, I can balance things in another way…although it is not like I was at home, but I can manage things (Guerreiro et al. 2004: 29).

Most of the interviewees felt privileged to work in a public organization, because, though not having a specific work–family policy, there is an attempt to follow the general legislation:

> And do you think that public services should help their workers to balance work and family affairs?

> I guess state, in this field, should give the example…to follow labour laws… if state doesn't give that example, no one will follow it. But, in this aspect, I guess we as public workers have some facilities…

> We have facilities in the sense we may be protected by legislation. In the private sector, what happens is that people can't even apply to legislation! (Guerreiro et al. 2004: 43).

In Portugal, there is a more protective law for public employees, defining a full-time job as 35 hours per week (Guerreiro et al. 2004: 10). Normal working hours at public sector are thus quite "short" compared to the long hours reported in the private sector organization.

A special policy, translated as "continuous journey" by the Portuguese research team, has been put in action in 1998: "If workers with special needs (studying, with children below 12, and so on) ask permission and justify their reasons, their employers should let them work 6 hours in a row, with no break for lunch (just half an hour used in the office). Doing so, workers may begin to work later or leave work earlier, extending their time for family affairs" (Guerreiro et al. 2004: 8).

Local services interpret and implement rules in a slightly different manner, according to their conditions and supervisor's policy. The policy of "continuous journey" was implemented in some services, while there were strong tensions about implementation in other places.

A key finding of the Portuguese case study in social services was that, similar to the situation in the UK, employee's knowledge about and use of their entitlements showed a great variation depending on one's job status. Low status employees (those with a low income and low education level) underlined that they are not entitled to any rights and privileges and considered themselves as discriminated.

The report identified four distinct situations depending on the work status. Managers demonstrate a great knowledge of public policies, but sometimes are against their full implementation. Regular intermediary workers have good knowledge of their rights and try to take advantage of all workplace policies. In contrast, low-skilled workers are not informed about new workplace policies and do not take advantage of them. Finally, temporary workers with individual work contracts are only partially included in services and are not able to take advantage of any workplace policies (Guerreiro et al. 2004: 29).

Wishes of Portuguese employees concerning better work–family reconciliation revolved around possibilities of reducing working hours, more flexible working hours, extended parental leave and more child care institutions:

> If you could make a wish to improve working parents' life, what would you ask?
>
> I'd like to work in part-time.
>
> Yes, it's true. And to extend maternity leave to one year. [...]
>
> Yes, at least, to give us flexible schedules. We might define our own schedule. [...]

And we need more institutions to care about our children. There are few [childcare institutions]

And to respect legislation! In my first leave, when I had my first child, they didn't give me my two hours per day for breast-feeding (Guerreiro et al. 2004: 49).

The Portuguese case study at social services showed that it could be characterized as a good workplace for parents since it was an organization concerned with following the legislation. However, many interviewees thought that in terms of generating autonomous policies to promote work–family balance (e.g. childcare services and flexibility of working schedules) there was a long way to go. A commonly stated wish of reducing working hours reflects the general unavailability of part-time work in the Portuguese labour market and the tradition of long working hours for both mothers and fathers (Sümer et al. 2008).

A General Comparison of Norwegian, British and Portuguese Social Services Case Studies with Respect to Work–Family Reconciliation

The Transitions project's case studies documented some similarities across the three workplaces. Social services in all three countries are female dominated organizations and are all going through important reorganizations. In all three countries jobs in the public sector are regarded as basically secure, however, reorganizations and budget cuts lead to a climate of growing insecurity. In all countries, parents employed in social services tend to compare their working conditions to those that prevail in the private sector organizations and think that their situation is better with respect to work–family reconciliation.

Especially in Norway and Portugal, the ease in making use of the "universal" rights laid down by national legislation is regarded as highly important for work–family reconciliation. Due to its basically non-interventionist legacy, the welfare state in the UK is not mentioned as a key actor in this field.

We could observe some important differences with respect to employees' knowledge of their entitlements between the countries. Policies that support work–family reconciliation (especially parental leave, sick child leave, flexitime and opportunities for part-time work) are well defined in the Norwegian legislation and are formulated as universal citizenship entitlements. Employees demonstrated good knowledge of their rights and existing work–family policies were extensively used and appreciated by Norwegian workers. In contrast, in Portugal and the UK many employees, and especially those in the lower levels of the hierarchy, lack basic knowledge about available policies (that are mainly induced by the EU) that could help them in reconciling work and family. Yet, our case studies also clarify a distinction between Portuguese and British contexts: While there is more expectation of welfare state involvement in this field among the Portuguese, the British have more individualized expectations. In the UK social services, managers were considered as key sources of support and constraint for work–family reconciliation. More understanding and flexibility from managers was an often stated wish of employed parents. Portuguese wished for better defined and implemented policies, especially related to opportunities to work part-time and childcare support. Norwegian social workers demonstrated the most politicized wishes that would make it easier for them to combine parenthood and employment, like a universal 6 hour working day and part-time work that would not result in disadvantages in the labour market.

Conclusions

The organizational case studies of the Transitions project which were based on focus group interviews conducted at workplaces supplied us with important contextual data to analyse how different family-friendly policies operate in practice. Work–family reconciliation has been an important topic on the EU social agenda and several Directives and Resolutions were formulated as reviewed in the former chapter. As a non-EU country, Norway belongs to the group of Nordic countries which pioneered the institutionalization of gender equality legislation focussing on the need to change the traditional division of care work, even though it was a late comer with respect to investment in public childcare for the youngest children. Norwegian working parents thus had entitlement for universally formulated parental leave policies with economic compensation from 1980s and significantly lengthened leave together with a fathers' quota from early 1990s. Norwegian parents have high expectations directed at the welfare state and especially demand improvements in the field of childcare since the supply of day-care services for the youngest children does not meet the demand (Sümer 2004). The high sense of entitlement of the Norwegian parents for public support in this field once again documents the importance of universally formulated benefits which was argued for by several other researchers in this field (e.g. Pascall and Lewis 2004, Brandth and Kvande 2001, Hochschild 1997, Anttonen 2002). Well institutionalized entitlements which do not demand individual negotiations prevent stigmatization and empower employees vis-à-vis their managers.

There have been changes in the parental leave schemes in both UK and Portugal following the EU legislation. Our case studies pointed up the important implementation gaps in this field. The three country comparison of work–family reconciliation experiences illustrated that these issues are still considered as more private in the UK, while Norway has a longer history of approaching them as public concerns. The Portuguese context is also characterized by an increasing pressure on families resulting in increasing expectations for public support.

The Transitions project also documented a key paradox related to gender equality: While part-time work and other flexible arrangements are promoted as benefits to support work–family reconciliation, the same package appears as the major reason behind the serious segregations in the labour market. As long as work–family policies target only women and are conceived as supports for working mothers, they risk contributing to an increased gender gap. A stronger emphasis on fathers' participation in childcare and on a more balanced sharing of care work is needed at various levels, both at national and European policy levels and within workplace practices.

Chapter 6
Concluding Discussion: Towards a European Gender Regime?

This book has explored different dimensions of European gender regimes with a focus on the complex interactions between paid work and care work. It has had a general objective of understanding how changes in gender relations are influenced by policies at different levels—EU, national and workplace—with a comparative perspective. The specific focus of the book was formed in the context of my personal biography as sketched in the Introductory chapter. My positioning as both an insider and outsider with respect to both the European Union and Scandinavia was a key element in defining the limitations, clarifying the theoretical perspective and carrying out the comparative analyses. The theoretical perspective adopted is an outcome of empirical findings of my earlier comparative studies of Turkey and Norway that called for a focus on the policy level. This perspective embraces a vision that gender equality is a matter of justice and that change is possible through collective action. The key question of how to formulate policies that will contribute to a more balanced distribution of power, time and wealth between men and women without contributing to an increase in other social inequalities has guided the theoretical reviews and empirical analyses. Methodologically, the book has been guided by an interdisciplinary, historically sensitive and case-oriented comparative approach.

In this concluding chapter, I will briefly review the key arguments developed in the former chapters in order to be able to consider their interconnections. This will be followed by a general discussion pertaining to the possibilities of promoting change with respect to gender through European Union legislation.

Chapter 2 offered a theoretical framework that guided the comparative approach. The arguments were structured around the productive dialogue between Esping-Andersen's analysis of the three welfare regimes and the massive feminist critique it triggered. The limited review in this chapter uncovered the impressive amount of intellectual production in this field.

What became clear was that an eye on the gendered division of unpaid work was indispensable in analysing gender policies and that we need to focus on policies, processes and outcomes simultaneously (Daly and Rake 2003).

What was most inspiring with Esping-Andersen's work is his move from a relatively gender-blind position to a clear acknowledgement of the centrality of gender relations in his later work. This is exemplified in his project in progress which is a book focussing on transformations in gender and generational relations. Even though many feminists are critical of certain aspects of his work, like his uncritical use of Hakim's controversial preference theory and his inadequate theorising of care related issues, many agree that his reworking of the original feminist concepts of defamilialization and women-friendly policy has been a welcome contribution. I would claim that Esping-Andersen contributed to gender mainstreaming by bringing mainstream theory closer to a gender-sensitive standpoint. This is reflected in his move from *The Three Worlds of Welfare Capitalism* (1990) in which women barely existed, to the venture of analysing *How Women Changed the World*.[1]

The review also made clear that the concepts of "welfare regimes" and "gender regimes" are powerful analytical constructs when employed carefully, to understand the developments at the macro scale. As "frameworks of power and rule" the "regime" concept has a great value in understanding complex and multidimensional forms of social inequality (Shaver 2000: 217). Yet we need to keep in mind that regimes are analytical constructs and individual countries often display ambiguities and complex transformations. The need to get into the field to investigate the specific contexts, carefully focussing on the gendered outcomes of different policies also became apparent in this review. Methodologically, this insight favours a comparative case study approach.

In this book, a strict categorization of "gender regimes" is avoided. Guided by Esping-Andersen's modified (more gender-sensitive) approach and selected feminist scholarship on the concept of gender regimes, a key differentiation among European countries is identified as their levels and forms of de-familialization. This involves an analysis of differences between countries with respect to their treatment of family related problems as private or public matters.

The countries are analysed mainly with respect to existing work–family reconciliation policies, availability of public support for childcare and formulation of the so-called "flexible" working arrangements. Three general groups can be identified based on this analysis:

- **Non-interventionist**: Work–family reconciliation is seen as an individual problem which can and should be solved by private (mainly market) solutions. Historically, the UK exemplifies this approach.
- **Familialistic**: Work–family reconciliation problems are addressed as

---

1   Title of Esping-Anderson's current book project as stated at his personal webpage: www.esping-andersen.com/.

family issues and families are basically left on their own to handle their problems. Family policies are undeveloped. Mediterranean countries, in varying degrees and forms, are good examples of this approach.
- **Defamilializing**: Work–family reconciliation is conceptualized as a public issue which can be solved by comprehensive public policies, such as subsidized and institutional childcare and secure parental leave for both parents. Nordic countries are the ones in which defamilializing policies are most developed and well institutionalized.

It is important to note that defamilialization does not imply "anti-family." Rather, it is the familialistic approach that appears as counter-productive to family formation (Esping-Andersen 1999: 67). The historically familialistic countries of Southern Europe struggle with the problem of low fertility, combined with lower rates of women in the labour market.[2] Defamilializing measures will help to decrease the burdens of working parents in combining their family and work obligations, especially by means of high quality and universally available childcare institutions. The relatively high fertility rates of Nordic women, combined with a high labour force participation rates of mothers, is often interpreted as an outcome of the defamilializing approach of the Scandinavian gender regime. The non-interventionist approach, namely defamilialization through markets, results in high social inequality and increased polarization. An increase in class inequalities is inherently against the original idea of "women-friendly" polity that seeks both gender and social equality.

"Refamilialization" measures, such as cash for home care, are used in several European countries, including Norway, France and Finland. Cash benefits are often framed as a means of ensuring "parental choice" (Mahon 2002). As discussed in the case study on Norway in Chapter 3, there are different feminist views on cash benefits. Many are critical of the rhetoric of "choice" taking the central place in policy discussions. Ellingsæter and Leira (2006) underline that gender-neutral policies advocating "choice" have gendered effects:

> In the everyday life of families with young children, 'choice' usually means *women* making the choices, that is, between paid employment and childcare […] The resources necessary for making a choice and the risks associated with it are, however, given little attention in public discourse (ibid.: 271, original emphasis).

Despite the shifts in policy discourse emphasizing choice and flexibility, the universalist traditions of the Scandinavian gender regime are still alive. Many studies show that a "gentle force" from the welfare state is needed to destabilize

---

2   Except in Portugal where women historically have a high rate of employment and tend to work long hours (Sümer et al. 2008).

the established gendered structures (e.g. Brandth and Kvande 2001). The famous fathers' quota in Norway and Sweden is the best example for this.

Different characteristics of the Scandinavian gender regime which is often referred to as the egalitarian alternative are discussed in many comparative studies. This led us to ask the question "is the Scandinavian Model a myth or is it real?"

Chapter 3 sought to discuss the accomplishments and pitfalls of the Scandinavian Model, focussing on three countries: Sweden, Denmark and Norway. The differences between these countries were downplayed to clarify some of the major characteristics of the institutions and policies for gender equality prevailing in all three. The key accomplishment of the model was characterized as the success in institutionalizing "women-friendly" policies (Hernes 1987) resulting in a "politicizing" of parenthood and childcare (Leira 2002; Ellingsæter and Leira 2006). Political parenthood involves a focus on the gendered division of care work and fathers' participation in childcare. Acknowledgement of childcare as a public responsibility and a social right is the key factor contributing to the widespread supply and demand of institutional and subsidised childcare services.

The analysis in Chapter 3 showed that there are several factors overshadowing the success of the model in achieving full gender equality. The highly segregated labour market contributes to women's higher economic vulnerability. Time use studies show that the gendered division of unpaid work has been stubborn to change. Although men have increased the time they spend for unpaid household work, women still use considerably more time on housework and childcare.

The detailed case study of Norway documented how Norway was the odd case with respect to childcare services in the 1980s and early 1990s and how this has changed leading to a characterization of the Norwegian family policy as "forward in all directions" in the 2000s (Ellingsæter 2003). But the current supply of public childcare places for the youngest children (aged 1 to 2) still lags behind the demand and this is reported as a major problem for working parents in many studies (e.g. Nilsen et al. 2004).

The speciality of the Scandinavian Model and its strong institutionalism became clearer when compared to countries that have a different welfare state model. Brief excerpts from my former comparative study of dual-earner couples from urban Turkey and Norway were used to illustrate this. When entitlements are universal and institutionalized, individuals tend to have clearly defined expectations directed at the welfare state and a clear conceptualization of their rights. With respect to work–family reconciliation, Norwegians rely heavily on public childcare and are critical of the lack of supply for the youngest children. Norwegian women, especially those with longer education, have relatively high fertility rates. In a European context characterized by below replacement fertility rate the combination of high fertility and many mothers in the labour market in Scandinavia led to a renewed interest in the Nordic welfare model. The possibility of combining active labour market participation with motherhood is enabled by a comprehensive policy package which also puts emphasis on changing the traditional division of childcare. These issues emerged on the EU social policy agenda throughout the 1990s and into the new Millennium.

Chapter 4 provided a critical account of the gender policies of the EU. A detailed analysis of the EU policy on work–family reconciliation and gender mainstreaming showed important accomplishments which are accompanied with backlash risks and ambiguities in this field. Both optimistic and pessimistic feminist views on EU policy were reviewed underlining a key north–south difference with respect to women's expected gains and losses. A key question was central in this review: Do economic concerns overshadow social and egalitarian concerns in the EU legislation?

This book signals a general belief in the project of the European Union, but emphasizes the need to preserve a critical eye on the neoliberal dominance and backlash tendencies. I believe that in imagining the future of Europe, there is a need to emphasize the qualities and strengths of "social Europe" vis-à-vis the marginal welfare model prevailing in the USA. The comparative analyses revealed the general need to intervene in the workings of the globalizing and "invisible" hand of the market, which apparently does not care about social justice or gender equality. In the attempt to change the gendered status quo, a focus on the complex interaction between gender relations and labour market practices is critical. Changing the image of the ideal worker from a mobile, independent, machine-like being to a gendered person with care responsibilities placed in a complex web of interdependence is a major task. Hopefully, this will be emancipatory for both men and women.

Is it realistic to expect a convergence in Europe with respect to changes in gender relations, both in the labour market and in the domestic sphere?

A European Gender Regime?

Feminist researchers are divided with respect to their evaluation of the EU. Those who are critical of the "equal opportunities" approach to the issue of gender equality think that EU gender policies are dominated by economic concerns formed with a neo-liberal orientation (e.g. Ostner 2000). The critics argue that policies which do not explicitly focus on the centrality of the gendered division of care work and the need to share family responsibilities end up becoming market-oriented policies that focus encouraging flexible forms of employment (Stratigaki 2004). Many emphasize the necessity of underlining the role of fathers and targeting policies in order to alter the established patterns of the gendered division of labour. Addressing different dimensions of gender regimes and their interactions is crucial:

> If gender equality policies are to be more effective in delivering equal treatment, in paid work and welfare, they need to address the interconnecting elements of gender regimes as systems, with a logic of gender equality in care work, income, time and voice, as well as in paid employment. This means developing an environment favouring more equal shares between men and women in paid work, care work, income, time, and voice, between individuals within households and in paid work and politics (Pascall and Lewis 2004: 380).

Being positive about the potentials of the EU, Walby (2004) argues that a distinct, "regulatory" gender regime is developing in the EU in which women's access to employment is facilitated by the removal of discrimination, regulation of working time to be compatible with caring and policies to promote social inclusion.

Some researchers argue that there is a convergence in European gender regimes and interpret this as a positive development. For example Von Wahl (2005) argues that three equal employment regimes exist in Western Europe and they have started to converge cautiously and in a nonlinear way toward a new EU standard: "The new EU level regime type is an outcome of the complex interplay among intergovernmental negotiation, suprantionalism, and recent innovations in governance, such as the open method of coordination" (von Wahl 2005: 85). According to von Wahl the EU made a progress towards recognizing women's difference:

> The 'reach and spread' of equal employment policies has moved *from* narrow *to* broad...The logic of the emerging EU equal employment regime expands *from* a limited sameness approach *to* the inclusion of women's difference (von Wahl 2005: 88, emphases original).

What is most important about the recent developments in the EU gender policy is that they contributed to bringing care related issues into the mainstream policy agenda underlining the necessity of intervention. As Pascall and Lewis (2004) emphasize, gender equality will belong to the better off unless care is underpinned with public services and regulation (ibid.: 385). Resort to the European Union legislation is especially needed in countries where women's movements are historically weak. The EU legislation can become an ally in making visible the unbalanced gendered division of labour as a matter of democracy and social inclusion. My positioning in two countries at the margins of the EU informs my cautious optimism.

From my Norwegian standpoint, I saw no great advantage specifically for Norwegian women to join the EU when the referendum was a hot topic on the political agenda in 1994. They already had a well institutionalized gender equality machinery. The issue of care work was already acknowledged as a public issue and what is more, was defined as a social right. In terms of gender equality and family policies, Norway was ahead of the EU's newly developing focus on work–family reconciliation and mainstreaming. But from my Turkish standpoint, I see clear advantages for Turkish women that a distant, but perhaps someday viable, membership in the EU will bring. The first step will be the focus on social inclusion and equal opportunities, which will bring issues related to gendered division of unpaid work onto the public agenda. I belong to the more optimistic group who believe that a mere discussion of these issues on the political agenda will eventually make a difference.

Another key issue pertaining EU legislation is the question of implementation. The different ways EU policies operated in practice were analysed in Chapter 5 based on qualitative data compiled through a large EU-funded project "Transitions." This project examined how young European men and women working in public and private sector workplaces manage work–family reconciliation in the contexts of different welfare state regimes, family and workplace support in eight European countries. Following a brief presentation of the key findings from different research phases, I focused on a more detailed analysis of work–family reconciliation practices based on case studies in selected units of national social services. Three countries, representing three different gender regimes (Norway, the UK and Portugal) were the focus of this analysis.

The analysis documented some similarities and important differences with respect to employees' experience of work–family reconciliation. In all three countries jobs in the public sector were regarded as basically secure, yet reorganizations and budget cuts lead to a climate of growing insecurity. Parents employed in social services tended to compare their working conditions to those that prevail in the private sector organizations and thought that their situation is better with respect to work–family reconciliation.

The ease in making use of the statutory rights was regarded as central for work–family reconciliation especially in Norway and Portugal. Due to the history of a highly private conceptualization of the family, the welfare state in the UK was not considered as a key actor in this field. While both UK and Portugal experienced a recent focus on work–family reconciliation policies induced by the EU, our case studies illustrated a distinction between these two contexts: While there was more expectation of welfare state involvement in this field among the Portuguese, the British continued to have more individualized expectations. In the UK social services, managers were considered as key sources of support and constraint for work–family reconciliation. More understanding and flexibility from managers was an often stated wish of the British working parents. Portuguese, on the other hand, often stated a wish of better defined and implemented policies, especially related to opportunities to work part-time and childcare support. In this comparison, Norwegian social workers demonstrated the most politicized wishes that would make it easier for them to combine parenthood and employment. A universal six hours work day and part-time work that would not result in disadvantages in the labour market were among those wishes. In all countries, working parents wished for more flexibility, conceiving it as an opportunity to decide on their working hours.

Paradoxes of Flexibility

The Transitions project contributed to a "deconstruction" of the concept of flexibility to understand its manifold usage by different actors. Flexibility can be time, space or work-contract related (Guerreiro et al. 2004). As a general pattern employer's and employee's definitions and expectations of flexibility differ. Employees tend to conceive flexibility as the possibility of controlling their own working hours. Employers, on the other hand, tend to focus on contractual flexibility, the ease of hiring and firing workers according to the needs of the organization. As documented by the Transitions project's case studies, contractual flexibility evident in the private sector and the trend towards individualization of contracts in many public sector organizations bring job insecurity. In the context of the intensification of work it can also lead to long working hours that intrude into family time or energy (Guerreiro et al. 2004)

Our analyses documented that flexibility is double-edged: It brings both opportunities and risks for employees. The Transitions study showed that working parents conceived flexibility related to their working time as an important support in their lives.

In her analysis of whether one of the key employment strategies of the EU, namely flexible working, is compatible with the policy objective of equal opportunities, Perrons (1999) argues that to the extent that flexible working builds upon and reinforces the prevailing domestic division of labour and financial dependency as a consequence of the pay and hours, then it is in conflict with the equal opportunities policies of the EU (ibid.: 412).

A large part of new jobs created consist of temporary and part-time employment and women are overrepresented in this type of work. These can be characterized as modern versions of female underemployment, reinforcing women's economic dependence (Rossilli 2000). Women are the majority among those employed in the "informal" sector and in these new "flexible" forms of employment. Perrons (1999) also asserts that women's overrepresentation in flexible work is consistent throughout the EU member states.

Empowering employees vis-à-vis managers in negotiating their caring responsibilities is of utmost significance as documented by the Transitions project data. The most effective way of achieving this is formulating collective solutions and universal entitlements that prevent stigmatization. It is a lot easier to ask for leave of absence for care related issues when everybody else is doing this. The high sense of entitlement prevailing in the Nordic countries exemplifies the power of this solution.

Universal benefits are the ones most compatible in achieving social inclusion. In concluding her analysis of the reconfiguration of work and family life, Crompton (2006) argues that statutory policies that support dual-earner families will at the same time reduce class inequalities (ibid.: 214). She also asserts the central role of collective solutions in the project of gender equality:

> Direct intervention (via statutory rights or other controls) in the employee-employer relationship would be unpopular with employers…and would work against the prevailing mood of the times…Nevertheless, it is likely to be necessary if contemporary societies are to effectively adapt to what has been one of the most significant social changes…the recognition and legitimacy of women's equal status to that of men (Crompton 2006: 218).

The issue is not importing the Nordic model to other European countries but showing the specific policy solutions that work well. The EU documents tend to use the concept of "good practices" as a suitable way of learning from the experiences in different contexts. Many comparative studies document the Scandinavian way of treating care related issues as public concerns as a distinctive good practice in the European context (Lewis and Smithson 2006).

The analysis and findings sketched above documented the need to reiterate the simple but equally powerful slogan of the women's movement from its early phases onwards: The personal is indeed political.

Turning Private Problems into Public Issues

The analyses in this book document the importance of discussing family-related problems as public issues. They promote a mobilization to bring childcare related problems on the social and political agenda.

The goals of gender equality and social inclusion are hard to achieve as long as gendered division of care work and work–family reconciliation problems are not discussed as major public and political issues. Treating these as "private problems" to be solved by individual solutions lead to a social polarization: privileged women depend on the unpaid or underpaid services of other women and manage to continue their labour market attachment and consequently the gendered division of work remains intact.

Policies focussing only on mothers' opportunities may contribute to a polarization among women:

> Policies enabling individual women to achieve equality with individual men— policies against sex discrimination, for parental leave, for equal opportunities —have brought women into the labour market and supported their ability to care for children. For women with higher education they have brought well-paid work and the capacity to pay for care. But they have created diversity in labour markets and in households, with gender equality accessible only to advantaged women. They have also brought gender equality to women on men's terms, enabling women to balance work and family, but offering no challenge to men to do the same (Pascall and Lewis 2004: 390).

As reviewed in detail in Chapter 4, the EU is promoting measures focussing on work–family reconciliation. But there are potential and emerging dangers preventing this policy from becoming a radical tool to promote gender equality. As Stratigaki (2004) rightly emphasized if reconciliation is not targeted specifically at men, it ceases to be an equality policy. This is what has happened in many European countries. Reconciliation became synonymous with offering flexible working conditions to women.

Another potential danger in work–family reconciliation rhetoric is the tendency of seeing care obligations as a "constraint" on labour (Daly and Rake 2003: 168) rather than promoting a mentality change in the labour market. The findings of the Transitions project which were discussed in Chapter 5 showed that reconciliation policies are often conceived as targeting only women. Another shortcoming is the exclusive emphasis on childcare, overshadowing other family obligations, like care of the elderly and other dependents.

Despite these concerns, the concept of reconciliation has been instrumental in bringing care related issues and the "private" life of the family onto the political agenda Europe-wide. Support for work–family reconciliation does not only imply providing childcare services in (public or private) institutions. It is about discussing care-related problems and gendered division of care work as public issues. Women need to have different options for combining motherhood and employment since "preferences" and opportunities will differ throughout the life course and with respect to specific working conditions. Being employed is not automatically leading to being empowered or independent. We need to design flexible enough policies that will allow for different combinations of child care and work involvement. However these entitlements need to be universal to prevent being stigmatized. Changing the gendered patterns in caring is essential and a key concern is finding a balance between the "masculinization" of the female life course and the strived feminization of the male life-course (Esping-Andersen 2002).

Targeting Fathers

This approach puts emphasis on the role of men in the project of establishing a more just division of power. This vision was formulated by Nancy Fraser (2000) as the "Universal Caregiver" model in which the welfare state would promote gender equity by dismantling the gendered opposition between breadwinning and caregiving:

> It would integrate activities that are currently separated from one another, eliminate their gender coding and encourage men to perform them too (Fraser 2000: 26).

In his new gendered approach to the welfare state restructuring, Esping-Andersen (2002) emphasizes the limits of the masculinization of the female life-course and asserts that

> ...ongoing change in gender behaviour is producing an increasingly 'masculine' profile on female biographies...The egalitarian challenge is unlikely to find resolution unless, simultaneously, the male life course becomes more 'feminine' (Esping-Andersen 2002: 70).

This means that men will also interrupt their attachment to the labour market to actively engage in the caring of their children and will be able to 'put the family first' when the demands of the two spheres clash.

It is important to challenge the hegemonic masculinity (Connell 1987) underestimating the role of fathers in the lives of young children. The right to claim reduced working hours or other flexible arrangements for childcare belongs to the fathers as well as the mothers.

Establishing fathers' paid leave of absence as a "normal" practice is an important step in working for this vision. Norway is a good case to study the possibilities and constraints related to this. Norwegian fathers' use of parental leave showed a dramatic pattern of upwards rise following the introduction of the fathers' quota. Currently, a great majority (around 85 per cent) of fathers use paternity leave. Qualitative studies on men's use of parental leave in Norway tend to document that this experience influences the ways men think about children's needs and care work in general (Sümer 2002). Studies also show that policies promoting father care are more significant on the symbolic level than on the level of actual division of labour between mothers and fathers (Lammi-Taskula 2006: 95). Although there are more pessimistic views on fathers' parental leave concerning the potential of this practice to make a real difference in the gendered division of household tasks, many feminists tend to acknowledge that fathers interrupting work even for a limited period of time to take care of their children has been a significant step.

The Scandinavian countries are the ones in the European context that came closer to this vision of promoting an egalitarian agenda based on universalistic entitlements and citizenship rights. The importance of developing public support for care is mentioned by several key contributors in the field. For example Pascall and Lewis (2004) maintain that "unless care is underpinned with public services, gender equality will belong to the better off. Secure care involves state provision as well as state and EU regulation" (ibid.: 385).

There are many arguments against the possibility of learning from the Scandinavian countries, mentioning the high cost of the Nordic model. I would argue that economic concerns do not need to be determining here since the key source for these policies is redistribution. Many different groups in society will accept paying moderate taxes when they are convinced that they will also benefit from the welfare network at some point in the course of their life. The key is establishing this vision as a realistic alternative and underlining that another system is possible. The egalitarian "individual earner-carer" (Sainsbury 1999) or the "universal caregiver (Fraser 2000)" model will be supported by large segments of European societies as long as it can be conceived as an option within the "horizon of legitimate expectations" (Marshall, quoted in Mahon 2002: 365).

Many crucial questions remain to be answered in light of new comparative studies: Is it possible to design flexible enough policies that would allow for different combinations of paid work and caring? How can universal policies adequately deal with the differences among groups of men and women?

Various studies show that the ideals and practices concerning work–family arrangements do not always match (e.g. Knudsen and Wærness 2001). Others point at the discrepancy between formal ideologies and everyday practices (e.g. Abrahamson et al. 2005). People's decisions and choices are structured by interacting influences of available state policies, cultural expectations and workplace dynamics. Preferences are shaped by what is conceived as available and available solutions depend on the structural and cultural mechanisms. Not many women would "choose" to confine themselves to a life-long commitment to the routines of housework if they had a real chance of getting a job in line with their capabilities which would also offer flexibility when the demands of the two spheres (namely the work and the family) clash. The meaning of work varies for women but few would disregard the importance of it as a source of economic independence and self confidence. Women vary with respect to their working time and working conditions. Some work part-time as a consequence of their own wish to spend more time with their children, while part-time and precarious work may be the only option for others. Thus, we need to challenge the tendency of treating all kind of employment as emancipatory and acknowledge that differences among women pose challenges for universalistic policies. The key issue is having a range of supporting policies that will give room for different work–family arrangements. We cannot talk about "preferences" with respect to the "choice" of working and mothering unless there are enough institutions that offer affordable and high quality childcare, combined with a reorientation at the societal level valuing care work, defining it as a social investment and encouraging men to participate.

Bibliography

Abrahamson, P., Boje, T. and Greve, B. (2005) *Welfare and Families in Europe*, Aldershot: Ashgate.

Andersen, J. G. and Hansen, P. (eds) (2002) *Changing Labour Markets, Welfare Policies and Citizenship*, Bristol: The Policy Press.

Andersen, T. B., Holmström, B., Honkapohja, S., Korkman, S., Söderstöm, H. T. and Vartiainen, J. (2007) *The Nordic Model: Embracing Globalization and Sharing Risks*, Helsinki: The Research Institute of the Finnish Economy.

Anttonen, A. (2002) "Universalism and Social Policy: A Nordic-feminist Revaluation" *NORA: Nordic Journal of Women's Studies*, 10(2): 71-80.

Beck, U. and Beck-Gernsheim, E. (1995) *The Normal Chaos of Love*, Cambridge: Polity.

Bergqvist, C. (1999a) "The Nordic Countries—One Model or Several?" in Bergqvist, C. et al. *Equal Democracies? Gender and Politics in the Nordic Countries*, Oslo: Scandinavian University Press.

Bergqvist, C. (1999b) "Childcare and Parental Leave Models" in Bergqvist et al. *Equal Democracies? Gender and Politics in the Nordic Countries*, Oslo: Scandinavian University Press.

Bergqvist, C., Borchorst, A., Christensen, A-D., Raaum, N. C., Ramstedt-Silen, V. and Styrkarsdottir, A. (eds) (1999) *Equal Democracies? Gender and Politics in the Nordic Countries*, Oslo: Scandinavian University Press.

Bergqvist, C. and Jungar, A-C. (2000) "Adaptation or Diffusion of the Swedish Gender Model?" in Hantrais, L. (ed.) *Gendered Policies in Europe: Reconciling Employment and Family Life*, London: Macmillan.

Boje, T. (2006) "Working Time and Caring Strategies: Parenthood in Different Welfare States" in Ellingsæter, A. L. and Leira, A. (eds) *Politicising Parenthood in Scandinavia: Gender Relations in Welfare States*, Bristol: Policy.

Booth, C. and Bennett, C. (2002) "Gender Mainstreaming in the EU: Towards a New Conception and Practice of Equal Opportunities?" *European Journal of Women's Studies*, 9(4): 430-446.

Borchrost, A. (1999) "Gender Equality Law" in Bergqvist et al. *Equal Democracies? Gender and Politics in the Nordic Countries*, Oslo: Scandinavian University Press.

Borchrost, A., Christensen, A-D. and Raaum, N. "Equal Democracies? Conclusions and Perspectives" in Bergqvist, C. et al. *Equal Democracies? Gender and Politics in the Nordic Countries*, Oslo: Scandinavian University Press.

Borchrost, A. and Siim, B. (2002) "The Women-friendly Welfare States Revisited" *NORA: Nordic Journal of Women's Studies*, 10(2): 90-99.

Bourdieu, P. and Wacquant, J. D. (1992) *An Invitation to Reflexive Sociology*, Cambridge: Polity Press.

Brandth, B. and Kvande, E. (2001) "Flexible Work and Flexible Fathers" *Work, Employment and Society*, 15(2): 251-267.

Castels, F. (2003) "The World Turned Upside Down: Below Replacement Fertility, Changing Preferences and Family-friendly Public Policy in 21 OECD Countries" *Journal of European Social Policy*, 13(3): 209-227.

CEDAW (2006) "Norway's seventh periodic report to the United Nations on Norway's implementation of the United Nations Convention on the Elimination of All Forms of Discrimination against Women (CEDAW)". Available online: http://www.regjeringen.no/en/dep/bld/Documents/Reports-and-plans/Reports/2006/Norways-7th-report-on-implementation-on-.html?id=424620

Cochrane, A., Clarke, J. and Gewirtz, S., (eds) (2001) *Comparing Welfare States*, London: Sage.

Connell, R. W. (1987) *Gender and Power: Society, the Person and Sexual Politics*, Cambridge: Polity Press.

Connell, R. W. (1990) "The State, Gender and Sexual Politics: Theory and Appraisal" *Theory and Society,* 19: 507-544.

Connell, R. W. (2002) *Gender*, Cambridge: Polity Press.

Cotter, Mooney A-M. (2004) *Gender Injustice: An International Comparative Analysis of Equality in Employment*, Aldershot: Ashgate.

Cousins, M. (2005) *European Welfare States: Comparative Perspectives*, London: Sage.

Dahl, H. M. and Eriksen, T. R. (2005) *Dilemmas of Care in the Nordic Welfare State: Continuity and Change*, Aldershot: Ashgate.

Daly, M. (2000a) *The Gender Division of Welfare: The Impact of the British and German Welfare States*, Cambridge: Cambridge University Press.

Daly, M. (2000b) "Paid Work, Unpaid Work and Welfare: Towards a Framework for Studying Welfare State Variation" in Boje, T. and Leira, A. (eds) *Gender, Welfare State and the Market: Towards a New Division of Labour*, London: Routledge.

Daly, M. (2005a) "Gender Mainstreaming in Theory and Practice" *Social Politics: International Studies in Gender, State and Society*, 12(3): 433-450.

Daly, M. (2005b) "Changing Family Life in Europe: Significance for State and Society" *European Societies*, 7(3): 379-398.

Daly, M. and Lewis, J. (2000) "The Concept of Social Care and the Analysis of Contemporary Welfare States" *British Journal of Sociology* 51(2): 281-298.

Daly, M. and Rake, K. (2003) *Gender and the Welfare State: Care, Work and Welfare in Europe and the USA*, Cambridge: Polity.

den Dulk, L., Peper, B. and Van Doorne-Huiskes, A. (2004) Transitions Research Report #2: *Literature Review* for the EU Framework 5 funded study "Gender, Parenthood and the Changing European Workplace" Manchester: Manchester Metropolitan University, Research Institute for Health and Social Change.

Duncan, S. and Pfau-Effinger, B. (2000) "Theorising Comparative Gender Inequality" in Duncan, S. and Pfau-Effinger, B. (eds) *Gender, Economy and Culture in the European Union*, London: Routledge.

Duncan, S. (2002) "Policy Discourses on Reconciling Work and Life in the EU" *Social Policy and Society*, 1(4): 305-314.

Duncan, S. and Pfau-Effinger, B. (eds) (2000) *Gender, Economy and Culture in the European Union*, London: Routledge.

EIRO (2006) "Reconciliation of Work and Family Life and Collective Bargaining in the EU", Available online: http://www.eiro.eirofound.eu.int

Eitrheim, P. and Kuhnle, S. (2000) "Nordic Welfare States in the 1990s: Institutional Stability, Signs of Divergence" in S. Kuhnle (ed.) *Survival of the European Welfare State*, London: Routledge.

Ellina, C. A. (2003) *Promoting Women's Rights: Politics of Gender in the European Union*, New York: Routledge.

Ellingsæter, A. L. (1999) "Dual Breadwinners Between State and Market" in R. Crompton (ed.) *Restructuring Gender Relations and Employment*, Oxford: Oxford University Press.

Ellingsæter, A. L. (2000a) "Welfare States, Labour Markets and Gender Relations in Transition: the Decline of the Scandinavian Model?" in Boje, T. and Leira, A. (eds) *Gender, Welfare State and the Market: Towards a New Division of Labour*, London: Routledge.

Ellingsæter, A. L. (2000b) "Scandinavian Transformations: Labour Markets, Politics and Gender Divisions" *Economic and Industrial Democracy*, 21(3): 335-359.

Ellingsæter, A.L. (2003) "The Complexity of Family Policy Reform: The Case of Norway" *European Societies*, 5(4): 419-443.

Ellingsæter, A. L. and Leira, A (2006a) "Introduction: Politicising Parenthood in Scandinavia" in Ellingsæter, A. L. and Leira, A. (eds) *Politicising Parenthood in Scandinavia: Gender Relations in Welfare States*, Bristol: Policy.

Ellingsæter, A. L. and Leira, A (2006b) "Epilogue: Scandinavian policies of parenthood—a success story?" in Ellingsæter, A. L. and Leira, A. (eds) *Politicising Parenthood in Scandinavia: Gender Relations in Welfare States*, Bristol: Policy.

Erikson, R., E. J. Hansen, S. Ringen, and H. Usitalo (eds), *The Scandinavian Model: Welfare States and Welfare Research*, New York: M. E. Sharpe.

Esping-Andersen, G. (1990) *The Three Worlds of Welfare Capitalism*, Cambridge: Polity.

Esping-Andersen, G. (1992) "The Three Political Economies of the Welfare State" in Kolberg, J. E. (ed.) *The Study of Welfare State Regimes*, New York: M. E. Sharpe.

Esping-Andersen, G. (1999) *Social Foundations of Postindustrial Economies*, Oxford: Oxford University Press.

Esping-Andersen, G. (2002) "A New Gender Contract" in Esping-Andersen, G. with Gallie, D., Hemerijck, A. and Myles, J. *Why We Need a New Welfare State* Oxford: Oxford University Press.

Esping-Andersen, G. and Korpi, W. (1987) "From Poor Relief to Institutional Welfare States: The Development of Scandinavian Social Policy" in Erikson, R. et al. (eds) *The Scandinavian Model: Welfare States and Welfare Research*, New York: M. E. Sharpe.

Esping-Andersen, G., Gallie, D., Hemerijck, A. and Myles, J. (2001) *A New Welfare Architecture for Europe?* Report submitted to the Belgian Presidency of the European Union.

European Commission (nd) Website of the Directorate General for Employment, Social Affairs and Equal Opportunities. Available online: http://ec.europa.eu/ social/main.jsp?catId=421&langId=en

European Commission (1996) Communication *Incorporating Equal Opportunities for Women and Men into all Community Policies and Activities*

European Commission (2005) *The Social Agenda 2005-2010: A Social Europe in the Global Economy: Jobs and Opportunities for All*, Directorate-General for Employment, Social Affairs and Equal Opportunities.

European Commission (2006a) *A Roadmap for Equality Between Women and Men 2006-2010* Communication from the Commission to the Council, the European Parliament, The European Economic and Social Committee and the Committee of the Regions.

European Commission (2006b) *Promoting Decent Work for All* Communication from the Commission to the Council, the European Parliament, The European Economic and Social Committee and the Committee of the Regions.

European Commission (2008) *Equality Between Women and Men, 2008.* Report from the Commission to the Council, the European Parliament, The European Economic and Social Committee and the Committee of the Regions.

Eurostat (2008) *The Life of Women and in Europe: A Statistical Portrait*, Luxembourg: Eurostat. Available online http://epp.eurostat.ec.europa.eu/ portal/page?_pageid=1090,30070682,1090_33076576&_dad=portal&_ schema=PORTAL

Fagnani, J., Houriet-Ségard G. and Bédouin, S. (2004), *Context Mapping* for the EU Framework 5 funded study "Gender, Parenthood and the Changing

European Workplace" Manchester: Manchester Metropolitan University, Research Institute for Health and Social Change.

Ferrera, M. (1996) "The 'Southern Model' of Welfare in Social Europe" *Journal of European Social Policy*, 6(1): 17-37.

Flax, J. (1990) "Postmodernism and Gender Relations in Feminist Theory" in Nicholson, L. (ed) *Feminism/Postmodernism*, New York: Routledge.

Fraser, N. (2000) "After the Family Wage: A Postindustrial Thought Experiment" in Hobson, B. (ed.) *Gender and Citizenship in Transition*, Houndmills: Macmillan.

Fraser, N. and L. Nicholson (1990) "Social Criticism without Philosophy: An Encounter between Feminism and Postmodernism" in L. Nicholson (ed) *Feminism/Postmodernism*, New York: Routledge.

Gender in Norway (nd) Information and Resources on Gender Equality and Gender Research in Norway. Available online: http://www.gender.no/

Giddens, A. (1984) *The Constitution of Society*, Cambridge: Polity Press.

Giddens, A. (1990) *The Consequences of Modernity*, Cambridge: Polity Press.

Giddens, A. (1999) *Runaway World: How Globalisation is Reshaping Our Lives*, London: Profile Books.

Gornick, J. C. and Meyers, M. K. (2004) "Welfare Regimes in Relation to Paid Work and Care" in J. Z. Giele and E. Holst (eds.) *Changing Life Patterns in Western Industrial Societies,* Elsevier Science Press.

Greve, B. (2007) "What Characterize the Nordic Welfare State Model" *Journal of Social Sciences*, 3(2): 43-51.

Guerreiro, M. das Dorres, Abrantes, P. and Pereira, I. (eds) (2004) *Case Studies Consolidated Report* for the EU Framework 5 funded study "Gender, Parenthood and the Changing European Workplace" Manchester: Manchester Metropolitan University, Research Institute for Health and Social Change.

Guerrina, R. (2002) "Mothering in Europe: Feminist Critique of European Policies on Motherhood and Employment" *European Journal of Women's Studies*, 9(1): 49-68.

Guillén, A. M. and Palier, B. (2004) "Introduction: Does Europe Matter? Accession to EU and Social Policy Development in Recent and New Member States" *Journal of European Social Policy*, 14(3): 203-209.

Gullestad, M. (1992) *The Art of Social Relations: Essays on Culture, Social Action and Everyday Life in Modern Norway*, Oslo: Scandinavian University Press.

Haas, B. (2005) "The Work-Care Balance: Is it Possible to Identify Typologies for Cross-National Comparisons" *Current Sociology*, 53(3): 487-508.

Haavio-Mannila, E. (1981) "The Position of Women" in Allardt, E. et al. (eds) *Nordic Democracy: Ideas, Issues and Institutions in Politics, Economy, Education, Social and Cultural Affairs of Denmark, Finland, Iceland, Norway and Sweden*. Copenhagen: Det Danske Selskap.

Hakim, C. (2006) "Women, Careers, and Work-Life Preferences" *British Journal of Guidance and Counselling*, 34(3): 279-294.

Hantrais, L. (1995) *Social Policy in the European Union*, New York: St. Martin's Press.

Hantrais, L. (ed.) (2000) "From Equal Pay to Reconciliation of Employment and Family Life" in Hantrais L. (ed.) *Gendered Policies in Europe: Reconciling Employment and Family Life*, London: Macmillan.

Hantrais, L. (2004) *Family Policy Matters: Responding to Family Change in Europe*, Bristol: The Policy Press.

Hantrais, L. (2005) "Combining Methods: A Key to Understanding Complexity in European Societies?" in *European Societies*, 7(3): 399-421.

Hartsock, N. (1990) "Foucault on Power: A Theory for Women?" in Nicholson, L. (ed.), *Feminism/Postmodernism*, New York: Routledge.

Hekman, S. (1990) *Gender and Knowledge: Elements of a Postmodern Feminism*, Cambridge: Polity Press.

Hernes, H. (1987) *Welfare State and Woman Power*, Oslo: Norwegian University Press.

Hirdman, Y. (1998) "State Policy and Gender Contracts: The Swedish Experience" in Drew, E. et al. (eds) *Women, Work and the Family in Europe*, London: Routledge.

Hobson, B., Lewis, J. and Siim, B. (eds) (2002) *Contested Concepts in Gender and Social Politics*, Cheltenham: Edward Elgar.

Hochschild, A. (1990) *The Second Shift: Working Parents and the Revolution at Home*, London: Piatkus.

Hochschild, A. (1997) *The Time Bind: When Work Becomes Home and Home Becomes Work*, New York: Metropolitan Books.

Hoskyns, C. (2000) "A Study of Four Action Programmes on Equal Opportunities" in Rossilli, M. (ed) *Gender Policies in the European Union*, New York: Peter Lang.

Humm, M. (1992) *Feminisms: A Reader*, New York: Harvester Wheatsheaf.

Jensen, A. (1999) "Partners and Parents in Europe: A Gender Divide" in Leira, A. (ed.) *Family Change: Practices, Policies and Values, Comparative Social Research*, 18, Stamford: Jai Press.

Kautto, M., Fritzell, J., Hvinden, B., Kvist, J. and Uusitalo, H. (eds) (2001) *Nordic Welfare States in the European Context*, London: Routledge.

Kautto, M. et al. (2001) "Introduction: How Distinct are the Nordic Welfare States?" in Kautto, M. et al. (eds) (2001) *Nordic Welfare States in the European Context*, London: Routledge.

Kitterød, R. H. (2002). "Mothers' Housework and Childcare: Growing Similarities or Stable Inequalities?" *Acta Sociologica: Journal of the Scandinavian Sociological Association*, 45(2): 127-149.

Kitterød, R. H. (2005) "Han Jobber, Hun Jobber, De Jobber: Arbeidstid Blant Par av Småbarnsforeldre" (*She Works, He Works, They Work: Working Time Among Couples with Small Children*), Statistics Norway Report 2005/10.

Kjeldstad, R. (2001) "Gender Policies and Gender Equality" in Kautto, M. et al. (eds) *Nordic Welfare States in the European Context*, London: Routledge.

Kleinman, M. (2002) *A European Welfare State? European Union Social Policy in Context*, Basingstoke: Palgrave.

Knudsen, K. and Wærness, K. (2001) "National Context, Individual Characteristics and Attitudes on Mothers' Employment: A Comparative Analysis of Great Britain, Sweden and Norway" *Acta Sociologica: Journal of the Scandinavian Sociological Association*, 44(1): 67-79.

Korpi, W. (2000) "Faces of Inequality: Gender, Class, and Patterns of Inequalities in Different Types of Welfare States" *Social Politics*, 7(2): 127-191.

Kumar, K. (1995) *From Post-Industrial to Post-Modern Society*, Oxford: Blackwell.

Lammi-Taskula J. (2006) "Nordic Men on Parental Leave: Can the Welfare State Change Gender Relations?" in Ellingsæter, A. L. and Leira, A. (eds) *Politicising Parenthood in Scandinavia*, Bristol: Policy Press.

Lappegård, T. (2003) "Pappa til (Hjemme)Tjeneste—Hvilke Fedre Tar Fødselspermisjon (Daddy to home service—which fathers take parental leave)" *Samfunnspeilet* (5): 49-55.

Leira, A. (1989) *Models of Motherhood: Welfare State Policies and Everyday Practices: The Scandinavian Experience*, Oslo: Institute for Social Research.

Leira, A. (1992) *Welfare States and Working Mothers: The Scandinavian Experience*, Cambridge: Cambridge University Press.

Leira, A. (1998) "Caring as Social Right: Cash for Childcare and Daddy Leave" *Social Politics*, 5(3): 362-378.

Leira, A. (2000). "Combining Work and Family: Nordic Policy Reforms in the 1990s" in Boje, T. and Leira A. (eds) *Gender, Welfare State and the Market: Towards a New Division of Labour*, London: Routledge.

Leira, A. (2002) *Working Parents and the Welfare State: Family Change and Policy Reform in Scandinavia*, Cambridge: Cambridge University Press.

Leira, A. (2006) "Parenthood Change and Policy Reform in Scandinavia, 1970s-2000s" in Ellingsæter, A. L. and Leira, A. (eds) *Politicising Parenthood in Scandinavia: Gender Relations in Welfare States*, Bristol: Policy Press.

Lewis, J. (1992) "Gender and the Development of Welfare Regimes" *Journal of European Social Policy*, 2(3): 159-73.

Lewis, J. (1997) "Gender and Welfare Regimes: Further Thoughts" in *Social Politics: International Studies in Gender, State and Society*, 4(2): 160-177.

Lewis, J. (2006) "Work/family Reconciliation, Equal Opportunities and Social Policies: the Interpretation of Policy Trajectories at the EU Level and the Meaning of Gender Equality" *Journal of European Public Policy*, 13(3): 420-437.

Lewis, J., Campbell, M. and Huerta, C. (2008) "Patterns of Paid and Unpaid Work in Western Europe: Gender, Commodification, Preferences and the Implications for Policy" *Journal of European Social Policy*, 18(1): 21-37.

Lewis, S. and Lewis, J. (eds) (1996) *The Work–Family Challenge: Rethinking Employment*, London: Sage.

Lewis, S. and Smithson, J. (eds) (2006) *Final Report* for the EU Framework 5 funded study "Gender, Parenthood and the Changing European Workplace" Manchester: Manchester Metropolitan University, Research Institute for Health and Social Change.

Lewis, S., Brannen, J. and Nilsen, A. (eds) (2009) *Work, Family and Organizations in Transition: A European Perspective*, Bristol: Policy Press.

Lister, R. (2006) "Gender, Citizenship and Social Justice in the Nordic Welfare States" in *NIKK* magasin (3), Oslo: Nordic Institute for Women's Studies and Gender Research.

Lombardo, E. (2003) "EU Gender Policy: Trapped in the 'Wollstonecraft Dilemma'?" in *European Journal of Women's Studies*, 10(2): 159-180.

Lombardo, E. and Meier, P. (2006) "Gender Mainstreaming in the EU: Incorporating a Feminist Reading?" in *European Journal of Women's Studies*, 13(2): 151-166.

Lombardo, E. and Meier, P. (2008) "Framing Gender Equality in the European Union Political Discourse" in *Social Politics* 15(1): 101-129.

Mahon, R. (2001) "Theorizing Welfare Regimes: Toward a Dialogue?" *Social Politics*, 8(1): 24-35.

Mahon, R. (2002) "Child Care: Toward What Kind of 'Social Europe'?" *Social Politics*, 9(3): 343-379.

Marshall, B. L. (1994) *Engendering Modernity: Feminism, Social Theory and Social Change*, Boston: Northeastern University Press.

Marshall, T. H. (1964) *Class, Citizenship and Social Development*, Chicago: University of Chicago Press.

Mazey, S. (1998) "The European Union and Women's Rights: From the Europeanisation of National Agendas to the Nationalisation of a European agenda?" in D. Hine and H. Kassim (eds) *Beyond the Market: The EU and National Social Policy*, London: Routledge.

Mills, C. W. (1959) *The Sociological Imagination*, New York: Oxford University Press.

Morgan, D. H. J. (1996) *Family Connections: An Introduction to Family Studies*, Cambridge: Polity Press.

Moss, P. (1996) "Reconciling Employment and Family Responsibilities: A European Perspective" in S. Lewis and J. Lewis (eds) *The Work–family Challenge: Rethinking Employment*, London: Sage.

Nilsen, A., Sümer, S. and Granlund, L. (2004): *Case Studies National Report: Norway* for the EU Framework 5 funded study "Gender, Parenthood and the Changing European Workplace", Department of Sociology, University of Bergen.

Nilsen, A. and Brannen, J. (eds) (2005) *Interview Study Consolidated Report* for the EU Framework 5 funded study "Gender, Parenthood and the Changing European Workplace" Manchester: Manchester Metropolitan University, Research Institute for Health and Social Change.

O'Connor, J. (1996) "From Women in the Welfare State to Gendering Welfare State Regime*s" Current Sociology*, 44(2).

O'Connor, J. S., Orloff, A. S. and Shaver, S. (1999) *States, Markets, Families: Gender, Liberalism and Social Policy in Australia, Canada, Great Britain and the US*, Cambridge: Cambridge University Press.

OECD (2007) "Babies and Bosses: Reconciling Work and Family Life" OECD Publishing.

OECD Factbook (2008) Available online: www.SourceOECD.org/factbook. 6 August 2008.

Oinonen, E. (2004) "Finnish and Spanish Families in Converging Europe" Electronic Dissertation, Tampere University Press.

Orloff, A. S. (1993) "Gender and the Social Rights of Citizenship: The Comparative Analysis of State Policies and Gender Relations" *American Sociological Review*, 58(3): 303-328.

Ostner, I. (2000) "From Equal Pay to Equal Employability: Four Decades of European Gender Policies" in Rossilli, M. (ed) *Gender Policies in the European Union*, New York: Peter Lang.

Pascall, G. and Lewis, J. (2004) "Emerging Gender Regimes and Policies for Gender Equality in a Wider Europe" *Journal of Social Policy*, 33(3): 373-394.

Perrons, D. (1999) "Flexible Working Patterns and Equal Opportunities in the European Union" *European Journal of Women's Studies*, 6(4): 391-418.

Pettersen, S. V. (2003) "Halvparten av Fedrene Vil ha Lengre Kvote" [Half of the fathers want a longer quota] in *Samfunnsspeilet*, 5: 39-49.

Pfau-Effinger, B. (2000) "Gender Cultures, Gender Arrangements and Social Change in the European Context" in Duncan, S. and Pfau-Effinger, B. (eds) *Gender, Economy and Culture in the European Union*, London: Routledge.

Pfau-Effinger, B. (2005) "Welfare State Policies and the Development of Care Arrangements" *European Societies*, 7(2): 321-347.

Powell, M. and Barrientos, A. (2004) "Welfare Regimes and the Welfare Mix" *European Journal of Political Research*, 43(1): 83-105.

Purcell, C., Lewis, S., Smithson, J. Caton, S. (2005) Transitions Research Report #7: *Report on Good Practice at Workplace Level in Supporting New Parents in their Paid Work and Family Life*. Report for the EU Framework 5 funded study "Gender, Parenthood and the Changing European Workplace" Manchester: Manchester Metropolitan University, Research Institute for Health and Social Change.

Rossilli, M. (2000) "The European Unions's Gender Policies" in Rossilli, M. (ed.) *Gender Policies in the European Union*, New York: Peter Lang.

Rydenstam, K. and Vaage, O. F. (2008) "Tidsbruk i Europeiske Land: Nordiske Menn Gjør Mest Hjemme (Time use in European Countries: Nordic men do most at home)" *Samfunnspeilet*, (1): 21-28.

Sainsbury, D. (ed.) (1994) *Gendering Welfare States*, London: Sage.

Sainsbury, D. (1999) "Gender, Policy Regimes and Politics" in D. Sainsbury (ed.) *Gender and Welfare State Regimes*, New York: Oxford University Press.

Saraceno, C. (2000) "Gendered Policies: Family Obligations and Social Policies in Europe" in Boje, T. and Leira, A. (eds) *Gender, Welfare State and the Market: Towards a New Division of Labour*, London: Routledge.

Shaver, S. (2000) "Inequalities, Regimes and Typologies" *Social Politics*, 7(2): 215-219.

Siim, B. (1987) "The Scandinavian Welfare States—Towards Sexual Equality or a New Kind of Male Domination?" *Acta Sociologica: Journal of the Scandinavian Sociological Association*, 30(3/4): 255-270.

Siim, B. (2000) *Gender and Citizenship*, **Cambridge University Press.**

Skjeie, H. and Siim,B. (2000) "Scandinavian Feminist Debates on Citizenship" in *International Political Science Review*, 21(4): 345-360.

Skrede, K. (1999) "Shaping Gender Equality—the Role of the State: Norwegian Experiences, Present Policies and Future Challenges" in Kitterød, H., Kjeldstad R., Noack, T. and Østby, L. (eds) *Livsløp i Støpeskjeen: Utvalgte arbeider av Kari Skrede*, Oslo: Statistisk Sentralbyrå.

Skrede, K. (2004) "Familiepolitikkens Grense—ved 'Likestilling Light'?" [The borders of family policy—at 'gender equality light'?] in Ellingsæter, A. L. and Leira, A. (eds) (2004) *Velferdsstaten og Familien: Utfordringer og Dilemmaer* (*The Welfare State and the Family: Challenges and Dilemmas*), Oslo: Gyldendal Akademisk.

Smart, C. and Neale, B. (1999) *Family Fragments?* Cambridge: Polity Press.

Smithson, J. and Lewis, S. (2005) Transitions Research Report #9. *National Debates on the Reconciliation of Family and Paid Work*. Report for the EU Framework 5 funded study "Gender Parenthood and the Changing Workplace" Manchester: Manchester Metropolitan University, Research Institute for Health and Social Change.

Solheim, J., and Ellingsæter, A. L. (eds) (2002). *Den Usynlige Hånd? Kjønnsmakt og moderne arbeidsliv* [The Invisible Hand? Gender power and the modern work life]. Oslo: Gyldendal.

SSB (Statistics Norway) (nd) Official statistics available online: http://www.ssb.no

SSB (2006) *Women and Men in Norway: What the Figures Say*, Oslo: Statistics Norway

Storvik, A. E. (2002). Hvorfår så få? Forklaringer på Mangelen på Kvinnelige Ledere [Why so few? Explanations for the lack of female leaders] *Søkelys på Arbeidsmarkedet*, 19(2), 253-259.

Stratigaki, M. (2005) "Gender Mainstreaming vs. Positive Action: An Ongoing Conflict in EU Gender Equality Policy" *European Journal of Women's Studies*, 12(2): 165-186.

Stratigaki, M. (2004) "The Cooptation of Gender Concepts in EU policies: The Case of Reconciliation of Work and Family" *Social Politics*, 11(1): 30-56.

Sümer, S. (1998) "Incongruent Modernities: A Comparative Study of Higher Educated Women from Urban Turkey and Norway" *Acta Sociologica: Journal of the Scandinavian Sociological Association*, 41:2, 115-29.

Sümer, S. (2002) *Global Issues/Local Troubles: A Comparative Study of Turkish and Norwegian Urban Dual-Earner Couples*. Bergen: Department of Sociology, University of Bergen.

Sümer, S. (2004) "Family and Gender Practices of Turkish and Norwegian Urban Dual-Earner Couples" *Sosiologisk Tidsskrift*, 12(4): 343-367, Oslo: Universitetsforlaget.

Sümer, S. and Nilsen, A. (2004) "Chapter 7: Norway" in den Dulk, L., Peper, B. and Van Doorne-Huiskes, A. (eds) *EU Research on Social Sciences and Humanities*, "Gender Parenthood and the Changing European Workplace: A State of the Art Report," pp. 167-191, Brussels: European Commission. Available online: http://www.cordis.lu/citizens/publications.htm ftp://ftp.cordis.europa.eu/pub/citizens/docs/transitions_eur21326_ok3.pdf.

Sümer, S., Granlund, L. and Nilsen, A. (2005) *National Report on Biographical Interviews: Norwegian Social Services*, for the EU Framework 5 funded study "Gender, Parenthood and the Changing European Workplace" Department of Sociology, University of Bergen.

Sümer, S., Smithson, J., das Dores Guerreiro, M. and Granlund, L. (2008) "Becoming Working Mothers: Reconciling Work and Family at Three Particular Workplaces in Norway, the UK and Portugal" *Community, Work and Family*, 11(4): 365-384.

Taylor-Gooby, P. (2001) "The Politics of Welfare in Europe" in Taylor-Gooby, P. (ed.) *Welfare States Under Pressure*, London: Sage.

Threlfall, M. (2000) "Taking Stock and Looking Ahead" in Hantaris, L. (ed.) *Gendered Policies in Europe: Reconciling Employment and Family Life*, London: Macmillan.

Tong, R. (1989) *Feminist Thought: A Comprehensive Introduction*, Boulder: Westview.

UNDP (1999) *Human Development Report*, United Nations Development Programme, New York: Oxford University Press.

Verloo, M. (2005) "Displacement and Empowerment: Reflections on the Concept and Practice of the Council of Europe Approach to Gender Mainstreaming and Gender Equality" *Social Politics*, 12(3): 344-365.

Von Wahl, A. (2005) "Liberal, Conservative, Social Democratic, or…European? The European Union as Equal Employment Regime" *Social Politics*, 12(1): 67-95.

Walby, S. (2004) "The European Union and Gender Equality: Emerging varieties of gender regime" *Social Politics*, 11(1): 4-29.

Walby, S. (2005) "Gender Mainstreaming: Productive Tensions in Theory and Practice" *Social Politics*, 12(3): 321-343.

Wallace, R. (ed) (1989) *Feminism and Sociological Theory*, London: SAGE.

Weintraub, J. (1997) "The Theory and Politics of the Public/Private Distinction" in Weintraub, J. and Kumar, K. (eds) *Public and Private in Thought and Practice: Perspectives on a Grand Dichotomy*, Chicago: University of Chicago Press.

Whelehan, I. (1995) *Modern Feminist Thought: From the Second Wave to "Post-Feminism"* Edinburgh: Edinburgh University Press.

Williams, F. (2008) "Introduction: The Challenge of Gender and Multiculturalism: Re-examining Equality Policies in Scandinavia and the European Union" *Social Politics*, 15(1): 1-4.

Wærness, K. (1987) "On the Rationality of Caring" in Sassoon, A. (ed.) *Women and the State: The Shifting Boundaries of Public and Private*, London: Routledge.

Wærness, K. (1998) "The Changing 'Welfare Mix' in Childcare and Care for the Frail Elderly in Norway" in Lewis, J. (ed.) *Gender, Social Care and Welfare State Restructuring in Europe*, Aldershot: Ashgate. pp. 207-228.

Wærness, K. (1998) "The Gender Division of Labour Between Norwegian Parents in the 1990s" in Hufton, O. and Kravaritou, Y. (eds) *Gender and the Use of Time*, Dordrecht: Kluwer.

Young, B. (2000) "Disciplinary Neoliberalism in the European Union and Gender Politics" *New Political Economy*, 5(1): 77-98.

Index